Modern Critical Interpretations

Eugene O'Neill's
The Iceman Cometh

Modern Critical Interpretations

These and other titles in preparation

Modern Critical Interpretations

Eugene O'Neill's
The Iceman Cometh

Edited and with an introduction by

Harold Bloom
Sterling Professor of the Humanities
Yale University

Chelsea House Publishers ◇ *1987*
NEW YORK ◇ NEW HAVEN ◇ PHILADELPHIA

© 1987 by Chelsea House Publishers, a division
of Chelsea House Educational Communications, Inc.,
   95 Madison Avenue, New York, NY 10016
   345 Whitney Avenue, New Haven, CT 06511
   5014 West Chester Pike, Edgemont, PA 19028

Introduction © 1987 by Harold Bloom

Printed and bound in the United States of America

∞ The paper used in this publication meets the minimum
requirements of the American National Standard for
Permanence of Paper for Printed Library Materials,
Z39.48-1984.

Library of Congress Cataloging-in-Publication Data
Eugene O'Neill's the iceman cometh.
   (Modern critical interpretations)
   Bibliography: p.
   Includes index.
   1. O'Neill, Eugene, 1888–1953. Iceman cometh.
I. Bloom, Harold. II. Series.
PS3529.N5I334   1987   812'.52   86-24443
ISBN 1-55546-048-8 (alk. paper)

Contents

Editor's Note

This book brings together what I take to be the best criticism yet devoted to Eugene O'Neill's *The Iceman Cometh*. The critical essays are reprinted here in the chronological order of their original publication. I am grateful to Rhonda Garelick for her aid in helping to locate and choose these essays.

My introduction begins by considering O'Neill's vexed relation both to American literary culture and to American society, and then proceeds to discuss *The Iceman Cometh* as a problematic instance of an American tragedy. Cyrus Day begins the chronological sequence by observing that the play is one of sheer nihilism, coming after the death of God. For Robert B. Heilman, the drama is kept just beyond the realm of tragedy by its author's despair.

In a more technical reading, Timo Tiusanen analyzes *The Iceman Cometh* as an interplay between protagonist and chorus. A social reading by Robert C. Lee shrewdly sees that evangelism and the Anarchist Movement serve the play as violent tropes for premature modes of disillusionment, a disillusionment that O'Neill judges us unable as yet to sustain.

Travis Bogard, contextualizing the play in the violent time of its original composition, just before the start of the Second World War, intimates that the despair involved was as much universal as it was O'Neill's more personally. In a more formalist study, Jean Chothia relates *Iceman*'s language and self-staging to its significant process of unfolding as dramatic revelation. John Orr, professedly sociological in approach, finds in the play a vision of O'Neill's rejection of the effect of capitalism upon American life.

In the final essay, Normand Berlin views *The Iceman Cometh* as redeemed from despair and nihilism by the quality of compassion it manifests. My introduction takes a rather different stance, and a juxtaposition of Berlin's judgment and my own should help to illuminate what remains problematic about one of O'Neill's strongest achievements.

Introduction

I

It is an inevitable oddity that the principal American dramatist to date should have no American precursors. Eugene O'Neill's art as a playwright owes most to Strindberg's, and something crucial, though rather less, to Ibsen's. Intellectually, O'Neill's ancestry also has little to do with American tradition, with Emerson or William James or any other of our cultural speculators. Schopenhauer, Nietzsche, and Freud formed O'Neill's sense of what little was possible for any of us. Even where American literary tradition was strongest, in the novel and poetry, it did not much affect O'Neill. His novelists were Zola and Conrad; his poets were Dante Gabriel Rossetti and Swinburne. Overwhelmingly an Irish American, with his Jansenist Catholicism transformed into anger at God, he had little active interest in the greatest American writer, Whitman, though his spiritual darkness has a curious, antithetical relation to Whitman's overt analysis of our national character.

Yet O'Neill, despite his many limitations, is the most American of our handful of dramatists who matter most: Williams, Miller, Wilder, Albee, perhaps Mamet and Shepard. A national quality that is literary, yet has no clear relation to our domestic literary traditions, is nearly always present in O'Neill's strongest works. We can recognize Hawthorne in Henry James, and Whitman (however repressed) in T. S. Eliot, while the relation of Hemingway and Faulkner to Mark Twain is just as evident as their debt to Conrad. Besides the question of his genre (since there was no vital American drama before O'Neill), there would seem to be some hidden factor that governed O'Neill's ambiguous relation to our literary past. It was certainly not the lack of critical discernment on O'Neill's part. His admiration for Hart Crane's poetry, at its most difficult, was solely responsible for the publication of Crane's first volume, *White Buildings*, for which O'Neill initially offered to write the introduction, withdrawing in favor of Allen Tate when the impossibility of his writing a critical essay on Crane's complexities became clear to O'Neill. But to have recognized Hart Crane's genius, so early and so helpfully, testifies to O'Neill's profound insights into the American literary imagination at its strongest.

The dramatist whose masterpieces are *The Iceman Cometh* and *Long Day's Journey into Night,* and, in a class just short of those, *A Moon for the Misbegotten* and *A Touch of the Poet,* is not exactly to be regarded as a celebrator of the possibilities of American life. The central strain in our literature remains Emersonian, from Whitman to our contemporaries like Saul Bellow and John Ashbery, and even the tradition that reacted against Emerson, from Poe, Hawthorne, and Melville through Gnostics of the abyss like Nathanael West and Thomas Pynchon, remains always alert to transcendental and extraordinary American possibilities. Our most distinguished living writer, Robert Penn Warren, must be the most overtly anti-Emersonian partisan in our history, yet even Warren seeks an American Sublime in his still-ongoing poetry. O'Neill would appear to be the most non-Emersonian author of any eminence in our literature. Irish-American through and through, with an heroic resentment of the New England Yankee tradition, O'Neill from the start seemed to know that his spiritual quest was to undermine Emerson's American religion of self-reliance.

O'Neill's own Irish Jansenism is curiously akin to the New England Puritanism he opposed, but that only increased the rancor of his powerful polemic in *Desire under the Elms, Mourning Becomes Electra,* and *More Stately Mansions.* The Will to Live is set against New England Puritanism in what O'Neill himself once called "the battle of moral forces in the New England scene" to which he said he felt closest as an artist. But since this is Schopenhauer's rapacious Will to Live, and not Bernard Shaw's genial revision of that Will into the Life Force of a benign Creative Evolution, O'Neill is in the terrible position of opposing one death-drive with another. Only the inescapable Strindberg comes to mind as a visionary quite as negative as O'Neill, so that *The Iceman Cometh* might as well have been called *The Dance of Death,* and *Long Day's Journey into Night* could be retitled *The Ghost Sonata.* O'Neill's most powerful self-representations—as Edmund in *Long's Day's Journey* and Larry Slade in *Iceman*—are astonishingly negative identifications, particularly in an American context.

Edmund and Slade do not long for death in the mode of Whitman and his descendants, Wallace Stevens and T. S. Eliot, Hart Crane and Theodore Roethke, all of whom tend to incorporate the image of a desired death into the great, triple trope of night, the mother, and the sea. Edmund Tyrone and Larry Slade long to die because life without transcendence is impossible, and yet transcendence is totally unavailable. O'Neill's true polemic against his country and its spiritual tradition is not, as he insisted, that: "Its main idea is that everlasting game of trying to possess your own soul by the possession of something outside it." Though uttered in 1946, in remarks before the first performance of *The Iceman Cometh,* such a reflection is banal, and represents a weak misreading of *The Iceman Cometh.* The play's true argument is that your own soul cannot be possessed, whether by possessing something or someone outside it, or by joining yourself to a transcendental possibility, to whatever version of an Emersonian Oversoul that you might prefer. The United States, in O'Neill's dark view, was uniquely the country that had refused to learn the truths of the spirit, which is that good and the means of good, love and the means of love, are irreconcilable.

Such a formulation is Shelleyan, and reminds one of O'Neill's High Romantic inheritance, which reached him through Pre-Raphaelite poetry and literary speculation. O'Neill seems a strange instance of the Aestheticism of Rossetti and Pater, but his metaphysical nihilism, desperate faith in art, and phantasmagoric naturalism stem directly from them. When Jamie Tyrone quotes from Rossetti's "Willowwood" sonnets, he gives the epigraph not only to *Long Day's Journey* but to all of O'Neill: "Look into my face. My name is Might-Have-Been; / I am also called No More, Too Late, Farewell." In O'Neill's deepest polemic, the lines are quoted by, and for, all Americans of imagination whatsoever.

II

Like its great precursor play, Strindberg's *The Dance of Death,* O'Neill's *The Iceman Cometh* must be one of the most remorseless of what purport to be tragic dramas since the Greeks and the Jacobeans. Whatever tragedy meant to the incredibly harsh Strindberg, to O'Neill it had to possess a "transfiguring nobility," presumably that of the artist like O'Neill himself in his relation to his time and his country, of which he observed that: "we are tragedy, the most appalling yet written or unwritten." O'Neill's strength was never conceptual, and so we are not likely to render his stances into a single coherent view of tragedy.

Whitman could say that "these States are themselves the greatest poem," and we know what he meant, but I do not know how to read O'Neill's "we are tragedy." When I suffer through the *New York Times* every morning, am I reading tragedy? Does *The Iceman Cometh* manifest a "transfiguring nobility?" How could it? Are Larry Slade in *Iceman* or Ed-

mund Tyrone in *Long Day's Journey into Night,* both clearly O'Neill's surrogates, either of them tragic in relation to their time and country? Or to
ask all this in a single question: are the crippling sorrows of what Freud
called "family romances" tragic or are they not primarily instances of strong
pathos, reductive processes that cannot, by definition, manifest an authentic
"transfiguring nobility?"

I think that we need to ignore O'Neill on tragedy if we are to learn
to watch and read *The Iceman Cometh* for the dramatic values it certainly
possesses. Its principal limitation, I suspect, stems from its tendentious
assumption that "we are tragedy," that "these States" have become the
"most appalling" of tragedies. Had O'Neill survived into our Age of Reagan
and observed our Yuppies on the march, doubtless he would have been
even more appalled. But societies are not dramas, and O'Neill was not
Jeremiah the prophet. His strength was neither in stance nor style, but in
the dramatic representation of illusions and despairs, in the persuasive imitation of human personality, particularly in its self-destructive weaknesses.

Critics have rightly emphasized how important O'Neill's lapsed Irish
Catholicism was to him and to his plays. But "importance" is a perplexing
notion in this context. Certainly the absence of the Roman Catholic faith
is the given condition of *The Iceman Cometh.* Yet we would do O'Neill's
play wrong if we retitled it *Waiting for the Iceman,* and tried to assimilate it
to the Gnostic cosmos of Samuel Beckett, just as we would destroy *Long
Day's Journey into Night* if we retitled it *Endgame in New London.* All that
O'Neill and Beckett have in common is Schopenhauer, with whom they
share a Gnostic sense that our world is a great emptiness, the *kenoma,* as
the Gnostics of the second century of the Common Era called it. But
Beckett's post-Protestant cosmos could not be redeemed by the descent of
the alien god. O'Neill's post-Catholic world longs for the suffering Christ,
and is angry at him for not returning. Such a longing is by no means in
itself dramatic, unlike Beckett's ironically emptied-out cosmos.

A comparison of O'Neill to Beckett is hardly fair, since Beckett is
infinitely the better artist, subtler mind, and finer stylist. Beckett writes
apocalyptic farce, or tragicomedy raised to its greatest eminence. O'Neill
doggedly tells his one story and one story only, and his story turns out to
be himself. *The Iceman Cometh,* being O'Neill at his most characteristic,
raises the vexed question of whether and just how dramatic value can survive
a paucity of eloquence, too much commonplace religiosity, and a thorough
lack of understanding of the perverse complexities of human nature. Plainly
Iceman does survive, and so does *Long Day's Journey.* They stage remarkably,
and hold me in the audience, though they give neither aesthetic pleasure
nor spiritually memorable pain when I reread them in the study.

For sheer bad writing, O'Neill's only rival among significant American authors is Theodore Dreiser, whose *Sister Carrie* and *An American Tragedy* demonstrate a similar ability to evade the consequences of rhetorical failure. Dreiser has some dramatic effectiveness, but his peculiar strength appears to be mythic. O'Neill, unquestionably a dramatist of genius, fails also on the mythic level; his anger against God, or the absence of God, remains petulant and personal, and his attempt to universalize that anger by turning it against his country's failure to achieve spiritual reality is simply misguided. No country, by definition, achieves anything spiritual anyway. We live and die, in the spirit, in solitude, and the true strength of *Iceman* is its intense dramatic exemplification of that somber reality.

Whether the confessional impulse in O'Neill's later plays ensued from Catholic *praxis* is beyond my surmise, though John Henry Raleigh and other critics have urged this view. I suspect that here too the influence of the non-Catholic Strindberg was decisive. A harsh expressionism dominates *Iceman* and *Long Day's Journey,* where the terrible confessions are not made to priestly surrogates but to fellow sinners, and with no hopes of absolution. Confession becomes another station on the way to death, whether by suicide, or by alcohol, or by other modes of slow decay.

Iceman's strength is in three of its figures: Hickman (Hickey), Slade, and Parritt, of whom only Slade is due to survive, though in a minimal sense. Hickey, who preaches nihilism, is a desperate self-deceiver and so a deceiver of others, in his self-appointed role as evangelist of the abyss. Slade, evasive and solipsistic, works his way to a more authentic nihilism than Hickey's. Poor Parritt, young and self-haunted, cannot achieve the sense of nothingness that would save him from Puritanical self-condemnation.

Life, in *Iceman,* is what it is in Schopenhauer: illusion. Hickey, once a great sustainer of illusions, arrives in the company of "the Iceman of Death," hardly the "sane and sacred death" of Whitman, but insane and impious death, our death. One feels the refracted influence of Ibsen in Hickey's twisted deidealizings, but Hickey is an Ibsen protagonist in the last ditch. He does not destroy others in his quest to destroy illusions, but only himself. His judgments of Harry Hope's patrons are intended not to liberate them but to teach his old friends to accept and live with failure. Yet Hickey, though pragmatically wrong, means only to have done good. In an understanding strangely akin to Wordsworth's in the sublime *Tale of Margaret (The Ruined Cottage)*, Hickey sees that we are destroyed by vain hope more inexorably than by the anguish of total despair. And that is where I would locate the authentic mode of tragedy in *Iceman*. It is Hickey's tragedy, rather than Slade's (O'Neill's), because Hickey is slain between right and right, as in the Hegelian theory of tragedy. To deprive the derelicts of hope is right, and to sustain them in their illusory "pipe dreams" is right also.

Caught between right and right, Hickey passes into phantasmagoria, and in that compulsive condition he makes the ghastly confession that he murdered his unhappy, dreadfully saintly wife. His motive, he asserts perversely, was love, but here too he is caught between antitheses, and we are not able to interpret with certainty whether he was more moved by love or hatred:

> HICKEY (*simply*). So I killed her. (*There is a moment of dead silence. Even the detectives are caught in it and stand motionless.*)
>
> PARRITT (*suddenly gives up and relaxes limply in his chair—in a low voice in which there is a strange exhausted relief*). I may as well confess, Larry. There's no use lying any more. You know, anyway. I didn't give a damn about the money. It was because I hated her.
>
> HICKEY (*obliviously*). And then I saw I'd always known that was the only possible way to give her peace and free her from the misery of loving me. I saw it meant peace for me, too, knowing she was at peace. I felt as though a ton of guilt was lifted off my mind. I remember I stood by the bed and suddenly I had to laugh. I couldn't help it, and I knew Evelyn would forgive me. I remember I heard myself speaking to her, as if it was something I'd always wanted to say: "Well, you know what you can do with your pipe dream now, you damned bitch!" (*He stops with a horrified start, as if shocked out of a nightmare, as if he couldn't believe he heard what he had just said. He stammers*) No! I never—!
>
> PARRITT (*to* LARRY—*sneeringly*). Yes, that's it! Her and the damned old Movement pipe dream! Eh, Larry?
>
> HICKEY (*bursts into frantic denial*). No! That's a lie! I never said—! Good God, I couldn't have said that! If I did, I'd gone insane! Why, I loved Evelyn better than anything in life! (*He appeals brokenly to the crowd*) Boys, you're all my old pals! You've known old Hickey for years! You know I'd never— (*His eyes fix on* HOPE) You've known me longer than anyone, Harry. You know I must have been insane, don't you, Governor?

Rather than a demystifier, whether of self or others, Hickey is revealed as a tragic enigma, who cannot sell himself a coherent account of the horror he has accomplished. Did he slay Evelyn because of a hope—hers or his— or because of a mutual despair? He does not know, nor does O'Neill, nor do we. Nor does anyone know why Parritt betrayed his mother, the anarchist activist, and her comrades and his. Slade condemns Parritt to a suicide's death, but without persuading us that he has uncovered the motive for so hideous a betrayal. Caught in a moral dialectic of guilt and suffering, Parritt appears to be entirely a figure of pathos, without the weird idealism that makes Hickey an interesting instance of High Romantic tragedy.

Parritt at least provokes analysis; the drama's failure is Larry Slade, much against O'Neill's palpable intentions, which were to move his surrogate from contemplation to action. Slade ought to end poised on the threshold of a religious meditation on the vanity of life in a world from which God is absent. But his final speech, expressing a reaction to Parritt's suicide, is the weakest in the play:

> LARRY (*in a whisper of horrified pity*). Poor devil! (*A long-forgotten faith returns to him for a moment and he mumbles*) God rest his soul in peace. (*He opens his eyes—with a bitter self-derision*) Ah, the damned pity—the wrong kind, as Hickey said! Be God, there's no hope! I'll never be a success in the grandstand—or anywhere else! Life is too much for me! I'll be a weak fool looking with pity at the two sides of everything till the day I die! (*With an intense bitter sincerity*) May that day come soon! (*He pauses startledly, surprised at himself—then with a sardonic grin*) Be God, I'm the only real convert to death Hickey made here. From the bottom of my coward's heart I mean that now!

The momentary return of Catholicism is at variance with the despair of the death-drive here, and Slade does not understand that he has not been converted to any sense of death, at all. His only strength would be in emulating Hickey's tragic awareness between right and right, but of course without following Hickey into violence: "I'll be a weak fool looking with pity at the two sides of everything till the day I die!" That vision of the two sides, with compassion, is the only hope worthy of the dignity of any kind of tragic conception. O'Neill ended by exemplifying Yeats's great apothegm: he could embody the truth, but he could not know it.

The Iceman and the Bridegroom

Cyrus Day

> *While the bridegroom tarried, they all slumbered and slept. And at midnight there was a cry made, Behold, the bridegroom cometh.*
>
> —MATT. 25:5–6

The Iceman Cometh is a play about the death of a salesman; its central theme is the relationship between men's illusions and their will to live. The salesman, Theodore Hickman, or Hickey, as he is called, is a more complex character than Arthur Miller's Willy Loman, and O'Neill's diagnosis of the spiritual *malaise* of the twentieth century is more profound than Miller's. Loman is depicted from the outside: he is the victim of a false and wholly external conception of what constitutes success. He wants, in a worldly sense, to solve the riddle of life, but the questions he asks are superficial and relatively easy for an audience or a reader to answer.

Hickey is depicted from the inside. He is more successful as a salesman than Loman, but he is the victim of a far more insidious disease. He is not versed at first hand (as O'Neill was) in philosophic nihilism, but he has somehow become aware, presumably through a sort of intellectual osmosis, that modern man no longer believes in objective reality and truth. Loman is adrift in contemporary American society; Hickey is adrift in the universe. The difference is a measure of the difference between O'Neill's aims and the aims of almost all other modern dramatists.

A few days before *The Iceman Cometh* opened on Broadway in 1946, O'Neill told a reporter that he had tried to express its "deeper" meaning in its title, and in an interview with S. J. Woolf he said that the verb form "cometh" was a "deliberate reference to biblical language." The play itself,

From *Modern Drama* 1, no. 1 (May 1958). © 1958 by A. C. Edwards.

he gave Woolf to understand, had religious significance. It is difficult to see what he can have meant by these hints, for *The Iceman Cometh* has few readily discernible connections either with religion or with the Bible. However, since O'Neill was not in the habit of talking at random about his own work, we would do well, if we want to come to terms with the "deeper" meaning of *The Iceman Cometh,* to assume that he had something specific and important in mind, and to try to discover what it was.

O'Neill looked upon himself, we must remember, as a spiritual physician, and he thought that his mission as a dramatist was to "dig at the roots of the sickness of today," which he defined as the death of the old God (echoing Nietzche) and the failure of science and materialism to provide a new one satisfactory to the remnants of man's primitive religious instincts. Most dramatists write about the relationship between man and man, but he was more interested, he said, in the relationship between man and God. His plays, accordingly, often have a metaphysical basis, but since he had lost his faith in God at an early period in his life, and since he thought that it would take a million years of evolution for man "to grow up and obtain a soul," they are seldom religious in any generally accepted sense of the word.

Days without End, which preceded *The Iceman Cometh,* is an exception. Written in 1934, during a brief period of personal happiness, it is a Christian play. The protagonist, a young man very much like O'Neill himself, is torn by religious doubts, but in the final act he enters a Catholic church, prostrates himself before an image of the crucified Jesus, and becomes at last an integrated personality, at peace with himself and with God. O'Neill, in 1934, appeared to have come to the end of his spiritual pilgrimage.

Actually, *Days without End* was a "mere interlude," as he admitted later, and did not reflect his personal religious convictions. For the moment he may have supposed that he could return to the Christian fold, but by 1939, when he wrote *The Iceman Cometh,* his mood had changed from tentative hope to unqualified despair. World War II was beginning, and the human race was obviously "too damned stupid" (this was O'Neill's phrase) to realize that its salvation depended on one "simple sentence": What shall it profit a man if he gain the whole world and lose his own soul? Perhaps, O'Neill told a reporter, mankind ought to be dumped down the nearest drain and the world given over to the ants.

These are hardly Christian sentiments, despite the quotation from the New Testament, and *The Iceman Cometh* cannot, therefore, have the same sort of religious significance as *Days without End*: it cannot be a Christian play. Can it be a recantation of the point of view of *Days without End*? Can it be, in any sense, a repudiation of Christianity?

Since O'Neill himself has given us the hint, let us begin our inquiry with the title. On the surface, the iceman is a reference to Hickey's ribald jest that he knows his wife is safe because he has left her with the iceman in the hay. On a "deeper" level, the iceman represents death, as O'Neill pointed out in 1946, and as Larry Slade points out in the play when he learns that Hickey's wife is dead. "It fits," Slade says, "for Death was the Iceman Hickey called to his home."

It is not enough, however, merely to identify the iceman with death. We must realize also that the iceman is the foil of the bridegroom of Scripture, and that he stands for the opposite of everything the bridegroom stands for. In the symbolism of theology, the bridegroom is always Christ, giver of life eternal. Waiting for the bridegroom symbolizes man's hope of redemption. Union with the bridegroom, conceived as a marriage, is the "final end and realized meaning" of the life of every Christian, "the fulfillment of promise and [the] consummation of hope." Union with the bridegroom signifies victory over death and salvation in the world to come.

Union with the iceman, conceived as adultery, must, then, be a parody of union with the bridegroom, and signify surrender to death and acquiescence in personal annihilation. Evelyn Hickman, after her husband kills her, finds the peace of oblivion in the arms of the symbolical iceman. The other characters in the play will eventually find the same kind of peace when they abandon their illusory hope of happiness, whether here and now on earth, or in a hypothetical Christian hereafter.

Construed in this way, *The Iceman Cometh* (on one of its many levels of meaning) is seen to be a parable of the destiny of man. All men are waiting for the iceman, but only those who have shed their ultimate illusions are aware that the "final end and realized meaning" of their lives is death. "I'm the only real convert to death Hickey made here," says Slade, who speaks for O'Neill in the play. "From the bottom of my coward's heart I mean that now."

"I want to go to the chair," says Hickey, when he realizes that his love for his wife was an illusion, and that he killed her because he hated her. "Do you suppose I give a damn about life now?" he asks the detective who has arrested him. "Why, you bonehead, I haven't got a single damned lying hope or pipe dream left." The other derelicts in Hope's saloon (the world of illusions) lack Slade's philosophic detachment and Hickey's psychopathic insight, and are afraid to face the truth: that waiting for the iceman constitutes the chief employment of their futile lives.

The paradox of fulfillment through annihilation is a concept that O'Neill could have derived either from Schopenhauer or from Freud, who reached the conclusion previously reached by Schopenhauer, though by a different route, that the goal of life is death. The immediate stimulus to his imagination, however, may have been Waldo Frank's novel *The Bridegroom Cometh,* in which the heroine gives herself to a succession of bridegrooms, both spiritual (Christ, Freud, Marx) and material (a husband and several lovers). Only Marx satisfies her need for love, and in the end she finds fulfillment through identification with the masses. O'Neill, unlike Frank, never supposed that a political or sociological nostrum could cure the diseases of the soul.

A second key to O'Neill's attitude toward Christianity in *The Iceman Cometh* is the role of the hardware salesman Hickey. When the curtain rises on act 1, the derelicts in Hope's hotel, slumbering and sleeping in their chairs, are waiting for Hickey to visit them on one of his periodical benders. "Would that Hickey or Death would come," says Willie Oban. But Hickey has tarried: a prostitute has seen him standing at the next corner, and to her surprise he is sober.

"I kidded him,"she says. "'How's de iceman, Hickey? How's he doin' at your house?' He laughs and says, 'Fine.' And he says, "Tell de gang I'll be along in a minute. I'm just finishin' figurin' out de best way to save dem and bring dem peace.' "

Hickey, when he arrives, is greeted by a very different cry from "Behold, the bridegroom cometh." "Here's the old son of a bitch," says Rocky; and "Bejees, Hickey, you old bastard, it's good to see you!" says Hope.

But Hickey is no longer the irresponsible drunkard the derelicts once knew and loved. He is on the wagon, and he proposes a stern remedy for what ails them. What he has to sell, in other words, is symbolical hardware, and he himself represents all self-appointed messiahs and saviors who meddle in other people's affairs and tell them how to live. Hence he can be fruitfully compared to Gregers Werle in Ibsen's *Wild Duck,* to Luka in Gorky's *Lower Depths,* and to the mysterious strangers in Jerome's *Passing of the Third Floor Back* and Kennedy's *Servant in the House.*

He also has something in common with Sigmund Freud, and his program of salvation is similar, in a general way, to psychoanalysis. He invites the derelicts to reexamine their pipe dreams (wish fulfillments) and to get rid of them by coming to terms with reality (the reality principle). This, he imagines, will make them happy. It doesn't, of course; and after their abortive attempts to resume their former occupations, they stagger back, demoralized and defeated, to the security of Hope's saloon. They cannot endure life unsupported by illusions, and instead of making them happy, Hickey deprives them of the will to live. Hickey has the last speech in each of the first three acts, and his last word in each is an ironical "happy." The notion that men can be happy in this worst of all possible worlds is an illusion.

Another illusion, or so Freud tells us, is religion. Man does not need its consolations, he says in *The Future of an Illusion,* nor can he remain a child forever. Rather he must venture out into the hostile world and be educated to reality. "Man can endure the cruelty of reality. What, you fear he will not stand the test? But it is at least something to know that one has been thrown on one's own resources."

This is very much like Hickey's program for the individual derelicts in *The Iceman Cometh.* Over and above their private illusions, however, stands Christianity, the collective illusion of what O'Neill thought of as our bankrupt Western civilization. Religion is an illusion, O'Neill evidently agreed; but unlike Freud, he did not think that the "swine called men" could live without it. Thus, by an extraordinary reconciliation of opposites, he equates the drunken Hickey with the secular savior Freud and the Christian Savior Christ, and at the same time rejects the gospels preached by both. Says Slade:

> Honor or dishonor, faith or treachery, are nothing but the opposites of the same stupidity which is ruler and king of life, and in the end they rot in the same grave. All things are the same meaningless joke to me, for they grin at me from the one skull of death.

That O'Neill had this anti-Christian undertone in mind when he compiled his medley of illusions in *The Iceman Cometh* is further substantiated by several tantalizing resemblances between the play and the New Testament. Hickey as savior has twelve disciples. They drink wine at Hope's supper party, and their grouping on the stage, according to O'Neill's directions, is reminiscent of Leonardo da Vinci's painting of the Last Supper. Hickey leaves the party, as Christ does, aware that he is about to be executed. The three whores correspond in number to the three Marys, and sympathize with Hickey as the three Marys sympathize with Christ. (The implications of this resemblance are not without precedent: Christopher Marlowe, it will be recalled, was accused of saying that the women of Samaria were whores.)

One of the derelicts, Parritt, resembles Judas Iscariot in several ways. He is the twelfth in the list of *dramatis personae;* Judas is twelfth in the New Testament lists of the Disciples. He has betrayed his anarchist mother for a paltry $200; Judas betrayed Christ for thirty pieces of silver. He is from the far-away Pacific Coast; Judas was from far-away Judaea. Hickey reads his mind and motives; Christ read Judas's. Parritt compares himself to Iscariot when he says that his mother would regard anyone who quit the "Movement" as a Judas who ought to be boiled in oil. He commits suicide by jumping off a fire escape; Judas fell from a high place (Acts 1:18) or "hanged himself" (Matt. 27:5).

In the light of O'Neill's remarks concerning the biblical and religious significance of his play, these resemblances can hardly be coincidental. They are no more than an undertone, to be sure—one of many undertones or subordinate layers of meaning—but they are consistent with the main theme of the play, and they account for some of its otherwise unaccountable features: for example, the emphasis on midnight (see Matt. 25:5–6) as the hour appointed for Hope's party, and the unnecessarily large number of derelicts in Hope's saloon. If O'Neill's only purpose had been to show that everyone, no matter how degraded, has one last pipe dream to sustain them, four or five derelicts, instead of twelve, would have sufficed, and the play would have been less redundant than, in fact, it is.

O'Neill was fond of hidden symbols and multiple layers of meaning. The nine acts of *Strange Interlude* and the name of the heroine, Nina, symbolize the nine months of a woman's pregnancy. Christine Mannon in *Mourning Becomes Electra* is called Christine (to correspond with Clytemnestra in Aeschylus's trilogy) instead of some other name beginning with "C" because O'Neill wanted to suggest that she is a sort of female anti-Christ or pagan martyr, crucified by a repressive Puritanism for her faith in sexuality. Lavinia Mannon is called Lavinia instead of a name beginning with "E" (to correspond with Electra) because "levin" means lightning or electricity. The name Mannon, from the last part of Agamemnon, suggests Mammon, the figurative divinity of all genuine Mannons. Examples of this sort of ingenuity, culled from other plays by O'Neill, could be multiplied indefinitely.

In addition to Hickey and Christine Mannon, O'Neill likens several other characters to Christ. In *The Fountain*, Bishop Menendez advises Juan to surrender the Indian Nano to the mob.

> JUAN (*with wild scorn*). Ah, High Priest! Deliver him up, eh?
> MENENDEZ. Juan! You are impious! (*Angrily*) It is sacrilege—to compare this Indian dog—you mock our Blessed Savior! You are cursed—I wash my hands—His will be done!

Nina, in *Strange Interlude*, cherishes the illusion that her dead lover Gordon Shaw is the real father of her son. "Immaculate conception," Marsden mutters in an unpublished manuscript version of the play. "The Sons of the Father have all been failures!" Nina says, referring both to her son and to Christ. "Failing, they died for us . . . they could not stay with us, they could not give us happiness."

Allusions such as these abound in O'Neill's plays. *Where the Cross Is Made,* to cite a final example, contains what I surmise is a double reference to the sustaining power of illusions (the central theme, as we have seen, of *The Iceman Cometh*). As the curtain falls on the last scene, Nat Bartlett cries out with insane frenzy: "The treasure is buried where the cross is made." On the surface, this means that Nat, like his father, is obsessed by the belief that the trinkets on the island represent a fortune in gold. But the words also suggest that Christianity, symbolized by the Cross, is as much of an illusion as the gold. In view of the way he worked and thought, O'Neill cannot have been unaware of this implication of his title.

These considerations bring to mind an ironic scene in *The Great God Brown.* Dion Anthony, one of O'Neill's favorite characters and a recognizable self-portrait, designs a cathedral which, he boasts, is "one vivid blasphemy from the sidewalk to the tips of the spires!—but so concealed the fools will never know! They'll kneel and worship the ironic Silenus who tells them the best good is never to be born!"

When Brown inherits Dion's soul, he too introduces secret motifs into his work. Of a new state capitol that he designs, he says:

> Here's a wondrous fair Capitol! The design would do just as well for a Home for Criminal Imbeciles! Yet to them, such is my art, it will appear to possess a pure common sense, a fat-bellied finality, as dignified as the suspenders of an assemblyman. Only to me will that pompous facade reveal itself as the wearily ironic grin of Pan as he half listens to the laws passed by his fleas to enslave him.

Did O'Neill, in writing *The Iceman Cometh*—the question inevitably presents itself—did O'Neill do what Dion and Brown do in *The Great God Brown?* Did he, that is to say, introduce concealed blasphemies into his play, just as Dion and Brown introduce concealed blasphemies into their architectural designs? And did he laugh in secret at the critics who supposed that he had written a compassionate play in *The Iceman Cometh,* just as Dion and Brown laugh at the fools who do not see through their mockery?

André Malraux once asked if man in the twentieth century could survive after God had died in the nineteenth. O'Neill's answer in *The Iceman Cometh* is no. The derelicts in Hope's saloon, all of them childless, symbolize a humanity that is engaged in the laudable act of committing suicide. As the play ends, Larry Slade stares straight ahead (O'Neill's habitual way of depicting disillusionment) and waits for release from the intolerable burden of life. O'Neill's prolonged search for a faith had led him, not to faith, but to despair.

Could there have been in 1939, a more prophetic anticipation of the self-destructive compulsions of the Age of Nuclear Fission? Is there in dramatic literature a more nihilistic play than *The Iceman Cometh?*

The Drama of Disaster

Robert B. Heilman

O'Neill's *The Iceman Cometh* (produced 1946) is a thematically much more complex work [than Maksim Gorky's *The Lower Depths*] in which the drama of disaster hovers on the border of tragedy, sometimes crosses the line, and might enter the tragic realm entirely if it were not for the restraining power of the author's despair. Yet, despite O'Neill's enrichment of the materials, his play has extraordinary resemblances to Gorky's, and these resemblances—between a Russian play and an American play four decades apart—will suggest the extensive modern concern with disaster. Both plays deal with a large and diverse group of disreputable or broken-down characters in a squalid rooming house, living in pasts or in hopes not really trusted, failing to break out (in each play lack of faith in human capabilities undermines a potential man-woman relationship that would involve getting away to another scene), finding relief in quarrel, cutthroat candor, and coma, waiting for a drinking bout such as appropriately ends each play, the crescendo of hilarity providing the background for the suicide of one man who has found his life intolerable. A still more striking parallel is the introduction into each underground pseudocommunity of an outsider with a remedial message, and the exploration, through him, of the doctrine of pity for human suffering; further, each volunteer savior evokes hostility.

But if one were making an issue of these resemblances—and there are other parallels of detail—he would also have to note the divergencies within the similar patterns. O'Neill's inmates are more decayed and sottish, more

From *Tragedy and Melodrama: Versions of Experience.* © 1968 by the University of Washington Press.

consistently dependent on "pipe dreams" (a key image), more deficient in brute vitality; fewer of them move also in the outer world; the disaster of personality is not attributed to social causes at all. The salvation-offering visitors from without are quite different in their theatrical and philosophic roles. In *The Lower Depths* Luka works on individuals in personal talks, adjusting his proffered help to each one's situation, whereas in *The Iceman Cometh* Hickey not only privately urges, but publicly and formally tries to force, everyone to accept his regimen. Luka, too mild to influence overt action, kindly encourages any faith, illusion, or belief that appears likely to contribute to an individual's well-being or comfort (heaven for the dying, a cure for the alcoholic, love and escape for the one pair that might have both); he says, "whatever you believe in, exists" (act 2). Hickey, a salesman with the "hard sell," relentlessly drives each man to test his illusions in action and thus to find that they are illusions; his program is the creation of absolute "peace" by the elimination of all pipe dreams.

Finally, the plays differ in the eventual dramatic "placing" of the evangelists. Though Luka arouses antagonism, the gambler Satine defends him in vigorous speeches evidently meant to have authority: Luka "lies" out of "sheer pity" for the weak and the parasitic, who "need lies"; truth is only for the strong and the free (act 4). And even in this constricted subworld there are bursts of animal vigor that are important in the dramatization of theme: they suggest the actual existence in the world—somewhere if not here—of the strength that can tolerate truth. But in O'Neill's play Hickey, the destroyer of illusion, is repudiated: his prospective beneficiaries reject him, and he is so characterized that the reader must reject him. This world is not divided into those who need pipe dreams and those who do not; rather the drama declares that the flight from reality is the absolute price of life. In O'Neill's depiction of victims, knowledge of self is disaster, for its leads to malicious enmity, brutal cynicism, suicide, murder; and peace, fellowship, and life depend on dream and drink.

Hickey presents himself as a man who can bring peace because he has found peace himself—by freeing himself from pipe dreams that have led to guilt and remorse. His pipe dream was that he would break away from a lifelong career of alcoholic and sexual binges; it was given sustenance by the constant forgivingness of his wife, and he freed himself from it, we gradually learn in a skillfully maintained process of revelation, by killing his wife. But at the same time this dream-destroyer tries to hold on to another pipe dream: that he loved and pitied his wife and wanted to give her peace. Then he trips himself up and falls suddenly into the realization that he hated her. (The situation is a remarkable anticipation of an episode recounted by the judge penitent in Camus's *The Fall* [1956]: a businessman faithless to a faithful wife "was literally enraged to be in the wrong, to be cut off from receiving, or granting himself, a certificate of virtue. . . . Eventually, living in the wrong became unbearable to him. . . . He killed her.") When Hickey finds out what he was really up to, he cries out that he hasn't "got a single damned lying hope or pipe dream left" and declares himself ready for "the Chair" (act 4). Our last view of Hickey is all irony: the anti-illusionist seeking to recover an illusion, and the madman desperately trying to think of himself, at his one moment of insight, as insane (he uses the word, or synonyms for it, seven times in the speeches before his final exit).

But the irony of Hickey's inconsistency, though it reinforces the theme and might in another play be of major consequence, is almost insignificant in contrast with the demonic, calculated irony on which the play turns: O'Neill's brilliant polemic stratagem of having the traditional castigation of the vice of self-deception, as well as the constructive counsels that might be given in psychotherapy, come from the mouth of a gross fornicator and a cunning salesman who has become a homicidal maniac. This old hand in vice—a meaner Iago, with a "magnetic personality," insight into human weakness, and skill in profiting from it—is given the coloring of a reformer and a do-gooder, even of the zealot who will force his medicines down the throats of those who he thinks need them. There could hardly be a more intensely hostile assault upon the doctrine that human salvation lies in discovering the truth and undergoing the pain that it may bring. In this drama of ideas O'Neill does not, however, betray his hand from the start: he does not get our backs up by immediately labeling the truth-bringer a phony and then simply playing for the cynical grimace at his falsity. Hickey is made initially plausible and draws us partly into his camp. Though a firm look at reality may seem a rather unpromising prescription for this barful of sodden wrecks, our beliefs are at least passively on Hickey's side, for it is possible that he may offer a key to betterment. Having been prepared to grant him "authority"—he has strength of personality, he makes some devastatingly sharp analyses of Larry Slade, the "philosopher" of the place, and he is able to act in the world—we then discover that he is a murderer and madman who, having wrecked his own life, must drive others into a similar destruction ("So you've got to kill them [dreams] like I did mine" [act 3]). O'Neill gets a maximum shock out of this—not to mention the delayed shock of our realization that he is defining the therapy of self-understanding as a cruel and vindictive fraud. And he seems clearly to desire the shock as a means of opening our eyes to his vision.

Yet this shock is not the same thing as the bald surprise of the slick popular play. In his dramaturgy O'Neill shows both competence and self-respect: the horror that is revealed in Hickey, though it has the force of a blow, is prepared for through two and a half acts before he confesses that he has shot his wife. The inmates abuse him in a variety of ways—as a liar, as a bringer of "bad luck," as being "not human," and, dozens of times, as being crazy and driving them crazy. Though these attacks are partly suspect because they originate in self-defensiveness, still they work cumulatively to make us ready for a truth not yet apparent. Our semiconscious doubt of his explicit objectives, and our readiness for the interpretation of him that O'Neill is finally to make, are most strongly influenced by the imagery of death that Hickey evokes in acts 3 and 4. That Hickey has "the touch of death" or "brings death" is said repeatedly by Larry Slade, the one derelict who still has a mind; then under Hickey's influence the men almost "murder" each other, Harry the proprietor feels and looks "like a corpse," and Hickey himself is worried because his patients "play dead." And in a brilliant grotesque modulation of the theme of death, the drinkers bitterly complain that the liquor itself "has no life in it": only after Hickey is dragged off to jail does it again make them forgetful and merry.

In his desire to universalize the action, O'Neill uses an infusion of allegory. One of the bums is known as "Jimmy Tomorrow," a metaphor for illusion that could be applied to most of the company. The proprietor is named Harry Hope; his sponging lodgers only too obviously "live on hope." Another device of universalization O'Neill might have got from Conrad—the wide distribution of the group by nationality, status, and former way of life. But one of O'Neill's problems is to convert his small barroom society into a microcosm, to make it seem something more than an enclave of ruin on all sides of which, however much out of sight, is a realm of normalcy. He does not, I believe, find a way of convincing us that he is picturing a representative humanity. Despite the powerful dramatization of theme, we are spectators a long way from the arena of disasters, held momentarily by shock and by a nightmarish distortion, but not drawn in by a sense of identity which art can make inescapable. Our separateness is, as always, a mark of an effect other than the tragic. We might be more drawn in if it were possible to feel in the play a larger theme: the theme that might be present is the defense of the life of myth, imagination, and faith against a dogmatic rationalism, the latter presented with diabolic cleverness as the revenge against society of the man who has lost his faith. But the range of the characters is too narrow for them to symbolize myth or reason successfully; it is difficult to think of Harry Hope's dependents as more than sick men or weaklings, and difficult—though perhaps less so—to think of Hickey as more than a quasi-rational scoundrel in a final vast project of the salesmanship that has always meant for him a slick psychological exercise of the power impulse.

Certain reminiscences of Conrad shed light on O'Neill's move away from the tragic toward the disastrous. O'Neill defends pipe dreams, and Conrad the dream; however, for O'Neill the pipe dream is simply an insulation against unbearable reality, while for Conrad the dream redeems the act, pulls man above the lowest level of conduct toward whatever virtues he can achieve. So Conrad believes that Lord Jim can endure the shame of his act of betrayal and can undergo a moral self-recovery and meet honorable death, whereas O'Neill clearly believes that for Don Parritt the only way out after his act of betrayal is a quick leap from the fire escape. Like Lord Jim, Parritt approaches a new knowledge in that he gradually surrenders the folds of deception with which for a time he has tried to hide the nature of his deed, but O'Neill's despair cuts off the wide range of experience that might follow when man stops lying.

Larry Slade, the ex-anarchist, and Axel Heyst in Conrad's *Victory* both cherish the illusion that they live in passive disillusionment on the shores of life, and both, in an interesting parallel, are ironically drawn into the stream by pity. Heyst learns that involvement means being overtaken by good as well as by evil, by love as well as by hate, and he acknowledges the guilt of retreat into inaction. Through pity, Larry defends the alcoholic dreamers against Hickey and in effect condemns Parritt to death as the only route from the sufferings of guilt to "peace." (Though with major differences, he parallels Gorky's Luka, who says, "Truth may spell death to you!" [act 2], "Truth doesn't always heal a wounded soul" [act 3], and who tells of a man who committed suicide when he lost faith in the actual existence of a "land of righteousness" [act 3].) Although in these ways and others Larry learns that actually he is not detached, he does not act (even too late); there is no galvanic shock of self-perception but only a gloomy acknowledgement of defeat in which it is difficult not to descry self-indulgence. "Be God, there's no hope! I'll never be a success in the grandstand—or anywhere else! Life is too much for me! I'll be a weak fool looking with pity at two sides of everything till the day I die!" (act 4). Larry's key phrases—"no hope" and "too much for me" and "weak fool"—reveal the artist looking at life in terms of victims, acted on rather than acting. This view of character is a clue to the sense of constrictedness that is frequently present, not only in O'Neill, but in the literature of disaster generally.

Composition for Solos and a Chorus: *The Iceman Cometh*

Timo Tiusanen

The Iceman Cometh fits the picture of O'Neill's development in many re-
spects. On his way toward his adolescence, toward the summer house in
New London, O'Neill stopped for a while in a New York saloon to visit
a group of friends he had known in the early nineteen-tens. On his way
toward three-dimensional characterization in serious plays, he left the triangle of *More Stately Mansions,* with its abstract Freudian elements, behind.
The derelicts in Harry Hope's "hotel" "call for a compassion and sympathetic understanding that is seldom aroused by Reuben Light or even the
Mannons." And on his way toward dynamic realism O'Neill has now both
the dynamics and the realism under control: behind the surface of realism
there is a purposeful patterning of the material, and the result might be
called a composition for the theatre.

Evidences of realism are apparent from the first, in the description of
the setting; the pendulum of the dynamics is put into motion in the characterization of the cast. "The back room is crammed with round tables and
chairs placed so close together that it is a difficult squeeze to pass between
them. . . . The walls and ceiling once were white, but it was a long time
ago, and they are now so splotched, peeled, stained and dusty that their
color can best be described as dirty." At the tables there is a motley crowd
of roomers, slumbering in the early morning hours. Nine of them are
furnished with the epithet "one-time" in the list of characters; Willie Oban
is, even more ironically, "a Harvard Law School alumnus." Thus the characters are given two roles, two masks right away: a contrast is immediately

established between what they are now and what they once were—and still believe they might be tomorrow.

The tension is further emphasized by what might be called a "yet," "but," or "still" quality, so common in O'Neill's descriptions of the outer appearance of his characters: "Still, he manages to preserve an atmosphere of nattiness and there is nothing dirty about his appearance"—Joe Mott, a Negro. "But despite his blubbery mouth and sodden bloodshot blue eyes, there is still a suggestion of old authority lurking in him like a memory of the drowned"—Piet Wetjoen, the Boer "General." "But his forehead is fine, his eyes are intelligent and there once was a competent ability in him"—James Cameron, one-time war correspondent, now "Jimmy Tomorrow." These and other contrasts are demonstrated in stage action and speeches from the moment the play opens, and its dialogue starts swinging.

Larry Slade, a pivotal character, sits at the table at left front in a prominent position. Larry's first role is that of a "Spielleiter"; he introduces the cast to Don Parritt, a newcomer. His second function is begun at the same time: he is to play unwilling confidant and finally executioner to Parritt, a tense eighteen-year-old boy, perhaps Larry's son, who has betrayed a group of anarchists to the police, among them his mother Rose. Why this happened is a carefully guarded secret, not to be revealed before the main action of the play reaches its climax—and this cannot even begin until Hickey, a jocular and profuse salesman, enters the scene to celebrate Harry Hope's birthday as he has always done.

He is eagerly expected all through act 1. While the characters are being introduced, they are also being organized into pairs and small groups. Within the total field of tension minor areas of local contact and conflict emerge. Larry, "the old Foolosopher" on his grandstand, pretends to have lost all faith and interest in life, especially in the Anarchist Movement to which he once belonged; he sits at the same table with Hugo Kalmar, a foreign-born anarchist, who periodically wakes up from his drunken stupor to denounce capitalism or sing snatches from a battle song. It is the year 1912: "General" Wetjoen, obviously of Dutch origin, is still fighting the Boer War against "Captain" Lewis, an obvious Englishman; they have a connecting link with Jimmy Tomorrow, correspondent in the same war. By gathering different nationalities into his cast O'Neill apparently aimed at a miniature of the American melting pot. Harry Hope, the benevolent proprietor of the saloon, is surrounded by two parasitic relatives, both "retired": Ed Mosher, a circus man, and Pat McCloin, a police lieutenant ousted from his job. The latter has a point of connection with Willie Oban, the law student, most advanced in his alcoholism. Joe Mott, the Negro, is most often alone among a white cast; he helps the bartenders, who have their private sources of income—Rocky keeps two streetwalkers, Chuck plans to marry his Cora.

These groups are played against one another and in parallel directions. Controlling a cast of twenty characters, among them a uniform group of ten roomers, would have been a difficult task if O'Neill had not employed these minor circles within the large one. The greatest common denominator between all characters is their belief in a delusion, a "pipe dream." Cora, Pearl, and Margie are just tarts, not whores; Rocky and Chuck are bartenders, not pimps; the roomers are firm in their belief in getting their old jobs back. There is thus a state of happy equilibrium in this "No Chance Saloon . . . , The End of the Line Café, The Bottom of the Sea Rathskeller"— until Hickey arrives.

He is a changed Hickey. He has given up drinking, and starts selling his new message with all the persuasiveness of an efficient salesman. It hits everyone on the stage where he is weakest. Away with the pipe dreams! cries Hickey. Why not face life as it is, without any delusions? Hickey has done so, and is now full of peace and contentment. He succeeds in spoiling Harry's birthday party beyond repair by telling them that his wife Evelyn is dead. Feelings of uneasiness and aggression start coming to the surface in act 3, after Hickey has spent all night convincing the others that it is necessary to realize one's pipe dreams in order to kill them.

The roomers come down and go out—in pairs, in small groups. The door of the bar is treated as the doors of the Mannon house and of the Harford summer-house were; there is thematic significance gathering around it. Only this time the intention is tragi-comic. Indoors the characters have found refuge; they are forced by Hickey to empty their stock of excuses and finally to enter the oppressing world outside. Last of all, to gain full advantage of the preceding repetitions, O'Neill lets Harry Hope cross the fateful threshold: he has not been outside since his beloved (and nagging) wife died twenty years ago. He is not outside long when an automobile, a novelty to him, nearly runs him over. At least this is how he tells it—not very convincingly. As in *Ah, Wilderness!* O'Neill employs a scenic unit used previously with tragic connotations to create comedy, here as an interlude in a tragedy.

All the time, the characters and events encountered by Hickey and Parritt bring these two closer to the final confession. At the end of act 3 Hickey tells his audience that Evelyn was murdered. Rocky and Larry have their misgivings; together with them we begin to suspect Hickey. Through these means O'Neill deliberately directs our attention to a specific question:

why? In a straightforward thriller the problem would be: who? All obstacles, half-truths, abruptly interrupted sentences, and the illusion of final peace and contentment are swept aside in Hickey's long modified monologue, face to face with those he wanted to save. He did not kill Evelyn because he wanted to spare her from further suffering as the wife of a hopeless victim to periodical drinking bouts; he killed her because he could not stand being forgiven any longer. In a sudden twist, where the voltage between love and hate is at its highest, Hickey reveals that he cursed his dead wife and her illusions of his amendment: "Well, you know what you can do with your pipe dream now, you damned bitch!" The confession, told "obliviously," is immediately followed by unconvincing persuasions of love; and Hickey's self-defensive remark that he must have been out of his mind is eagerly accepted by the roomers. If they can believe that Hickey has been insane from the beginning, they can safely return to their old dreams. So they do; all except Parritt, who is forced by Hickey's example into a parallel confession. He commits suicide, the only relief granted to him by Larry. His body hits the ground on the backyard shortly before the roomers, as a final touch of irony, begin singing in a drunken chorus, each a different song. O'Neill's composition closes with a cacophony, out of which a French Revolutionary song sung by Parritt's fellow anarchist, Hugo Kalmar, emerges victorious.

The Iceman Cometh is essentially a series of modified monologues. They are intertwined and counterpointed, until the final impression is far from static; and their material is richer than in More Stately Mansions. There are numerous stage directions in which O'Neill remarks that his characters speak out of inner compulsions and that the listeners are inattentive. Parritt goes on "as if Larry hadn't spoken"; Hickey speaks "staring ahead of him now as if he were talking aloud to himself as much as to them." These are the two characters in whom the inner compulsions are too strong to be subdued by any amount of resistance, not even that furnished by a stage full of antagonistic listeners. Willie Oban and Hugo Kalmar, on the other hand, have the minimum amount of restraint: they emerge from their drunken stupor to shout their thoughts and pass away again. The others are in between; yet all are given an opportunity to reveal their characteristic fluctuation between two different masks.

The dynamics within the speeches are part of the reason why O'Neill was now capable of relying on his dialogue more than ever. The speeches are written in his native tongue—the American vernacular. The changes in the visual stage picture are kept to a minimum: there are three settings, all depicting the same bar with minor variations in the angle. It is worth noticing that even here O'Neill remained truthful to his circle structure: acts 1 and 4 have the same setting, with a small but significant change in the placement of the chairs, emphasizing Hickey's lonely position. The impression of immobility is further accentuated by keeping stage action to a minimum; most of the time, all the characters are on stage, sitting solidly in their chairs. All these "demobilizing" factors help to keep the attention of the audience focused on O'Neill's music-like handling of his themes.

On the next level, there is an interaction between different characters and groups of characters. Rosamond Gilder in her review of the original production of *The Iceman Cometh* states: "There is little movement; there is only an antiphonal development of themes. . . . O'Neill's bums . . . spend most of their time in blissful or tormented alcoholic slumber. O'Neill uses this device to bring them in and out of the action without making them leave the stage. As the play progresses, the way the tables are grouped in the backroom and bar and the manner in which actors are grouped around them—slumped over asleep or sitting in a deathly daydream—provides a constant visual comment on the developing theme." Within the realistic framework there is a thematic fluidity which would not be permitted in a tighter play, closer to the formulas of the "well-made play." The coordinating factor is a problem common to all characters—not a plot, in which each should perform his own, highly individual function. The significance of the plot had been diminishing in O'Neill ever since *Ah, Wilderness!*, another indication that *Days without End* and not the comedy was a digression. *The Iceman Cometh* is, in its orchestral organization of the material, O'Neill's *The Three Sisters*.

The problem of length arises out of necessity. As a matter of fact, it has been actual ever since *Strange Interlude*; *Mourning Becomes Electra,* a "plotty" and straightforward play, was not as open to criticism as O'Neill's long postwar plays. There is full reason to refer again to the paradox of the O'Neillian length—a paradox seemingly so easily solved with the help of a blue pencil.

There are circumstances that speak for cautiousness when shortening the mature O'Neill. A certain speech may not carry any theme—but perhaps it helps to create atmosphere. A detail is repeated eighteen times—yet perhaps this kind of piling up is part of the playwright's total plan. What happens to the composition if whole movements are dropped out? It is conceivable that the criterion of those most eager to shorten O'Neill has been a play with a tightly knit plot. *The Iceman Cometh* is a play of another kind. On the other hand, a music-like handling of the themes is not one of the first associations an outsider makes when seeing a collection of bums sitting in their "last harbor"; it is possible that someone hears only the words "pipe dream," not the themes persistently carried by them. All in all, I am ready to leave the shortening to the stage directors who know their theatre and their cast and have their own interpretation of the play—hopefully, a profound one. In other words, Gassner is right: some of the repetitiveness "can be removed without injury to the play."

Gassner has also spoken of the "cyclopean" architecture of *The Iceman Cometh*. There is definitely an architecture behind it; even if the action seems to be transferred freely from group to group, from character to character, the play's total structure is carefully planned. It is the director's task to evoke the total atmosphere; it is not his task to call attention to the underlying scheme. There are sudden reversals in the mood of the play: Hickey receives a spirited welcome, then his transformation arouses bafflement; his toast to Harry in the birthday party is greeted by "an enthusiastic chorus," then he mentions the words "pipe dream," and "in an instant the attitude of everyone has reverted to uneasy, suspicious defensiveness." One of the pipe dreams that keeps the play swinging from one harbor to another is that insults and revelations are only "kidding." The dynamics are under control; the twists are motivated both psychologically and structurally. Comedy is used to build up tragedy.

Waith has described the whole movement of the play by comparing it to "the advance and retreat of a huge wave." It begins with the characters in a torpor, it ends with their "slipping back into drunken stupor; only three of them have been flung free of the wave—Hickey, Parritt, and Larry." The same characters are selected by Tom F. Driver as the core of *The Iceman Cometh*: "The play might be diagrammed with three concentric circles. In orbit on the outer circle are the numerous characters who inhabit Harry Hope's bar, including Harry himself." Larry and Parritt, who do not return to their previous state of existence, are "in a circle within the outer one," while Hickey "occupies the play's innermost circle" and his own story "is virtually a play within the play and . . . the core of the entire business."

After these structural considerations, we are ready to concentrate on the central chorus scenes in *The Iceman Cometh*. It is O'Neill's last group play; as in his previous efforts within the limits of this genre, he is primarily interested in the relations between an individual and a uniformly reacting mass of people. There is interaction, not only within the speeches and within and between minor groups of characters, as indicated above; there is also interaction between Hickey and the roomers, and this tension is partly responsible for the most memorable scenic image in the entire play—the moment of Hickey's confession.

Driver is right: Hickey is the protagonist of *The Iceman Cometh*. Not all critics have drawn this conclusion. Engel writes: "The protagonist, Larry, also serves a choral function as he comments upon the action and interprets the motives of the numerous other characters"; he is echoed by Doris V. Falk. If we say that the protagonist serves a choral function, the elements of Greek tragedy get confused, and the result is a contradiction in terms. This would not be so harmful, it if were not in this particular case apt to conceal certain central features of the play. For there is a chorus in *The Iceman Cometh,* and there is a protagonist playing against this chorus: Hickey against the roomers.

This is not the first time O'Neill employed one or several choruses. *The Moon of the Caribbees, The Emperor Jones, The Hairy Ape,* and *Marco Millions* included chorus scenes, until the line of development reached its climax in the exuberant arias and "choral odes" of *Lazarus Laughed.* After that, the group of townspeople was utilized with restraint in *Mourning Becomes Electra,* at the beginning of each play. In *The Iceman Cometh* the chorus is still more fully integrated into the fabric of the play: chorus members are simply actors with different roles to perform. They are gathered into a chorus in two key scenes, at the end of acts 2 and 4; these scenes are prepared for by the group scene at the close of act 1.

Obviously, this is a dramatic not a lyric chorus. Yet it is possible to draw functional parallels to Greek practice. Lucas writes about the general task of the Athenian chorus: "It provides the poet with a mouthpiece, and the spectator with a counterpart of himself. It forms a living foreground of common humanity above which the heroes tower." In their refusal to listen to Hickey's story the roomers express the natural abhorrence shared by the audience. Following their temporary chorus leader, Harry Hope, they denounce the towering hero of the play: "Hope: Get it over, you long-winded bastard! . . . (*A chorus of dull, resentful protest from all the group. They mumble, like sleepers who curse a person who keeps awakening them, 'What's it to us? We want to pass out in peace!'*)" They are not "wasps, birds, frogs, goats, snakes," nor more fantastically "clouds, dreams, cities, seasons"; they are drunkards. Or, if a more fantastic interpretation is allowed within the realistic framework of the play, we come close to one of the roles listed above: they are pipe dreams.

More specifically, O'Neill seems to be closest to the functions given to the chorus by Sophocles. In a well-known passage of his *Poetics* Aristotle recommends the dramatic function: "The chorus should be treated as one of the actors, should be an integral part of the whole, and should participate in the action, not as in the plays of Euripides but as in those of Sophocles."

Most specifically, O'Neill moves close to the functions given in the *Antigone* and the *Oedipus Tyrannus*: "When Creon, in the *Tyrannus,* enters in indignation, the chorus is there to receive him, but the scene gains enormously in effectiveness from the fact that it thus begins on a level of neutrality, from which it can gradually work up to its violent close." In *The Iceman Cometh* the role of the chorus begins on a level of friendship and eager acceptance, from which it can gradually work up to the level of antagonism and hatred—until the final, ironical twist brings back the friendly atmosphere. O'Neill was not satisfied with one swing of the pendulum: he made it turn back again, to add to the dynamics of the play.

It is important to emphasize both the functional parallels and the formal discrepancies. O'Neill employs the chorus of the roomers much less literally than the several choruses in the pretentious sequences in *Lazarus Laughed* located in antique Greece and Rome. Hickey has sixteen listeners in both of the chorus scenes, in the latter only after the arrival of the two policemen; this is one more than the prescribed fifteen—if Larry is not interpreted as "the second actor." Whether this conjecture is correct or not has no bearing on the effectiveness of the chorus scenes. Any of the choreutae can be made to leave this function and carry with his individuality a fragment of one of the themes. The movements are mainly mental; the reactions are described with precision (even the silences are recorded). The role of the choryphaeus is alternately occupied by several characters, occasionally by Larry or even Chuck, most consistently by Harry Hope. The first of the chorus scenes is more fluid and less intense than the finale; short interruptions in the conversation between Hickey and the chorus are possible in both—in act 2 Willie even sings his song. When Hickey approaches his final confession, the intensity of the scene increases and the interpolations become shorter: the protagonist eats, as it were, the role of the chorus, in spite of its collective efforts.

O'Neill mentions the word "chorus" several times in his stage directions; yet its decisive function in the total dynamics of *The Iceman Cometh* has hardly been recognized emphatically enough. This time O'Neill did not seek for added scope by employing literary parallels; he employed devices of the theatre. Everything in the play is made to concern a whole group of characters, and this group is drawn together into a chorus which forms a background for the soloists. Hickey's sudden reversal from pretended love to real hatred reverberates much more strongly than any of the fluctuations in *More Stately Mansions* simply because his modified monologue is addressed to a stageful of characters, all reacting to the speech, if not otherwise, at least by keeping silent. They are a continuous visual and

aural commentary on the monologue; this is the scene in which the illus-
trating function of the secondary characters, mentioned by Gilder, has its
greatest impetus. Nor is O'Neill alone among the modern dramatists to
employ various modifications of the antique chorus; T. S. Eliot, Jean
Giraudoux, Sean O'Casey, Bertolt Brecht, and Friedrich Dürrenmatt share
his company, the last in *The Visit,* where the chorus scenes proceed toward
greater tightness and intensity, as they do in *The Iceman Cometh.* What is
even more important than distinguished company is that the chorus is made
an intricate part of O'Neill's play, of its dynamics. It does not imitate the
outer form of the Greek chorus; it repeats its accentuating function. The
solos and the chorus sing the same melody.

The acute observations on the structure of *The Iceman Cometh* put forth
by Driver have been quoted above; they are supported by scenic evidence,
by the grouping of the characters in act 4. Driver also mentions the functions
of the secondary characters as a chorus. Later on in his study, he drifts to
rather doubtful conclusions via *A Touch of the Poet.* He senses in that play
a kind of distrust in art, in the creations of human imagination. According
to this line of thought, O'Neill was interested in art only as a formula for
philosophical quest: "he was not concerned with art as form, or if he was
so, only negatively, as a matter of pure necessity. . . . His vocation of
writing plays was not followed for the purpose of achieving the best possible
plays, the right forms incarnating the right conceptions, but rather for the
purpose of using the writing to wrestle with life itself. . . . [His work] is
weak at almost every point where we care to ask an aesthetic question."

Driver's aesthetics apparently do not include the art of the theatre, for
this is where O'Neill's plays are strong at almost every point. A man who
is "not concerned with art as form" does not write masterpieces; after *The
Iceman Cometh* O'Neill completed another, *Long Day's Journey into Night.*
Nor did he renounce every aspect of his past in *The Iceman Cometh,* as
Engel assumes: "he repudiated not only love, faith and truth but also, by
implication, that to which he had dedicated his life: the theatre itself de-
pending as it is upon the willing acceptance of illusion." O'Neill's dedication
to the theatre is written on every page of his canon, not by any means
excluding the late climax; the speculations of Driver and Engel are unnec-
essary. O'Neill might have been separated from the theatre of the late thirties
and forties, but he was not estranged from his personal means of expression,
tried and conquered during thirty years of restless and vigorous experimentation. Now, approaching the end of his career, he masters them.

A fallacy of another kind is to deny all development in O'Neill's last
plays. A primary exponent for this opinion was Miller, who said in 1962:

"There was really nothing new. Only two plays had previously been unseen, and they showed nothing beyond extreme length (this was old hat)
and heavy-handed 'realism' (an early O'Neill trademark)." It is remarkable
that the word "realism" is furnished with apostrophes, as an indication of
uncertainty. It *is* a vague word: it means hardly anything because it means
almost anything. It is a concept in the history of literature, denoting a phase
in the development of the novel after Flaubert; Gassner calls it "Modern
Classicism" in drama, and any recent best-selling novel is acclaimed for its
"harsh realism." In the middle of this confusion all one can do is to furnish
this vague word with some additional epithet; that is why I have termed
O'Neill's late style "dynamic realism." The point to be made is that there
is something new in his postwar plays, that it would have been utterly
impossible for the young O'Neill to write *The Iceman Cometh, Long Day's
Journey into Night, A Moon for the Misbegotten*, or even *A Touch of the Poet,*
closest of these to conventional realism.

How much inner movement there is in the "heavy-handed realism"
of *The Iceman Cometh* has, hopefully, been shown above. The speeches
would be static without the special device of modified monologue, combined with masks; the masks of past and present open up the dimension of
time; the drama would not proceed without its courageous music-like handling of the themes and of groups of characters; and the play would lack
dynamics without the chorus, a scenic unit O'Neill learned to utilize during
his excursions into Greek tragedy. *The Iceman Cometh* is based on the results
of O'Neill's experimental period; these are now presented in new
modifications.

Robert F. Whitman has noticed a connection between fluctuation in
the states of mind and the liberal use of spirits in O'Neill's postwar plays:
"Liquor . . . serves two functions: it permits the dramatist to show the
contrast between a man sober, with his defenses up, and drunk, when his
subconscious drives become overt, and allows the rapid juxtaposition of
contradictory moods and impulses once a person *is* drunk. It is a device
which O'Neill uses for much the same purposes as the more radical in-
novations, to reveal the conflicts which tear his characters apart and frustrate
their potentialities as complete human beings, without appearing arbitrary
or mechanical."

These observations are ingenious, especially because Whitman recognizes the connection between O'Neill's earlier "radical inventions" and
the more cautious, yet dynamic later style. A play in which a similar method
is used is *Mr. Puntila and His Hired Man, Matti* (Herr Puntila und sein Knecht
Matti) by Brecht and Hella Wuolijoki. The above quotation has full validity
in the case of *Long Day's Journey into Night;* elsewhere, it is perhaps pushed

a little too far. There is no drinking at all in *More Stately Mansions,* a play Whitman was not familiar with; and it is not so much liquor as the lack of it, combined with Hickey's dogged preaching, that makes the derelicts of *The Iceman Cometh* reveal themselves. In *A Touch of the Poet* Nora and Sara disclose their innermost thoughts when under mental pressure; it can be said that pressure of some kind is the primary reason for fluctuation. Liquor (and morphine) are, to be sure, used in several cases as a realistic motivation and as an additional impetus. Modified monologues, with their inner compulsions, hark far back in O'Neill.

More Stately Mansions helps to reveal the central theme and a central weakness in *The Iceman Cometh* more clearly than before. In a way, the later play can be called a direct continuation of the cycle play. *More Stately Mansions* ends with a choice: Simon decides to kill one of his pipe dreams, to escape the intolerable conflict between two vectors within his personality by regressing into childhood. When *The Iceman Cometh* begins, Hickey has made his choice; the play shows what follows—death. It is as if O'Neill had left only two alternatives to man, one tragic, the other dishonest. Relieve the tension and die; try to deal with it in the best possible way by ignoring it, and go on living and dreaming. There is powerful irony in the last minutes of the play, when Hickey is taken away and the roomers return to their pipe dreams. The choice is precisely described by the Finnish poet Uuno Kailas in his lapidary lines from 1931: "*Vain kaks on ovea mulla, / kaks: uneen ja kuolemaan*" ("I have but two doors, / but two: to the dream and to death").

Yet O'Neill is not so much concerned about the pipe dreams as such as about their influence on our neighbors. He does not condemn the roomers; he pities them. His judgment of those who impose their dreams on people they love is harsher. Sara's dream of more stately mansions spurs Simon forward along the wrong road; Deborah needs her little boy Simon to fulfill her dreams. Evelyn's stubborn belief in Hickey's ability to "stay on the wagon" is presented as the basic reason for his tragedy; and things only went from bad to worse when Hickey started to preach his new message. Selling all kinds of ideologies, including the ideology of complete disillusionment, leads only to aggression and to death, as the happy equilibrium is destroyed. O'Neill had recently recovered from the disturbing effects of the ideology of Nietzscheism on his art; perhaps the Anarchist Movement is referred to so many times only as "the Movement" in order to give it a kind of general validity. *The Iceman Cometh* is a counter-sketch of O'Neill's own *Lazarus Laughed.*

Seclusion, Deborah's private hell in *More Stately Mansions,* is now seen as the only comfortable form of existence. The themes of isolation and non-communication are even given a comic treatment in the role of Harry Hope, who pretends to be half-blind and half-deaf: "Can't hear a word you're saying. You're a God-damned liar, anyway!" The reconciliatory tones are devoted to the roomers who do not disturb anyone with their dreams. Hickey is a tragic hero: he neither asks nor receives any reconciliation after his self-recognition.

This is how the basic relation between the protagonist and the chorus, between an individual and the common mass of mankind can be seen in *The Iceman Cometh*. The tragic figure is placed in the middle of this world of ours, not quite without its comedy; it is his task to choose between the absolutes, between love and hatred, life and death. Leech calls the play "a comedy with tragic overtones"; rather, it is a tragedy with comic overtones. Hickey even fits in with the Aristotelian formula, if this is given a fairly wide application: he is given stature by the chorus, by great expectations, by his function as a savior. His social position is high in comparison with the other characters on the stage. This is all that any playwright gives us: relative stature in a microcosm. Hickey is the one-eyed king in the country of the blind.

The weak spot of the play is Larry. He is a descendant of Simon who does too much preaching and attitudinizing; his role may lead to an overpowering temptation to abridge. Fortunately, he was not made the protagonist of *The Iceman Cometh*. It is as if Larry's problem—to pity or not to pity?—had been too closely personal to O'Neill: the playwright himself had recently decided to pity, but could not help continuing to dispute the point in the play, somewhat aside from its center. This state of mind was fruitful for writing a tragedy, however, with its combination of two necessary ingredients, pity and grimness. A tragedian, not reconciled to existence as it is, sees grimly and pityingly disharmonies and conflicts between human absolutes, such as life and death, love and hatred, guilt and innocence, then exaggerates and stylizes them for the good of his play. Part of the controversies among critics start at the point when the permissible degree of exaggeration and stylization are to be judged: shall there be people of eminent social stature involved? Can there be human dignity in Harry Hope's saloon? There can; and a katharsis is achieved, perhaps through the purgation of pity and fear, whatever this means, more probably through a comprehension of the playwright's vision. In *The Iceman Cometh* O'Neill is a much better tragedian than in *More Stately Mansions*, left to us as a torso. In the finished play his vision is more generally valid, his form less contrived, his mastery over the scenic means of expression more complete.

Evangelism and Anarchy
in *The Iceman Cometh*

Robert C. Lee

With O'Neill one must always go back to *The Iceman Cometh,* for it is both his culmination and his demise. *Long Day's Journey into Night* and *A Moon for the Misbegotten* follow it, but more for personal purgation than art. *Long Day's Journey* sums up O'Neill's life, while *Iceman* sums up all life. "The *Iceman* is a denial of any other experience of faith in my plays," O'Neill said in 1946. Earlier, in 1940, he had said, "There are moments in it that suddenly strip the secret soul of a man stark naked." As always, that naked soul was O'Neill himself.

For all its over-criticized length, *Iceman* is a play that has yielded but slowly. Perhaps its sledgehammer nihilism has acted to block, indeed confuse, understanding. There has been, for instance, fairly widespread carping because the drunks in Harry Hope's saloon do not get drunk in any normal way. Similarly, it has sometimes been bruited about that the spiritual hardware salesman, Hickey, goes mad at the end of the play. Eric Bentley, without question the leading detractor of *Iceman,* has mitigated his attacks in recent years, but not by passing through the maze that *Iceman* is. In his introduction to the play in *Major Writers of America,* Bentley surmises that the play "ought to have been about Hickey's unresolved Oedipus complex," but it could not because "O'Neill's Oedipus complex was unresolved. That at least is the interpretation which I wish to submit for discussion." Bentley's former colleague at Columbia, Robert Brustein, in *The Theatre of Revolt,* concludes his discussion by saying, "*The Iceman Cometh,* then, is about the impossibility of salvation in a world without God." If so, then what of

From *Modern Drama* 12, no. 2 (September 1969). © 1969 by A. C. Edwards.

love, that other fundamental impossibility in the O'Neillian world of icemen?

The play could be worked through O'Neill's life; that too has been tried. John Mason Brown even conjectured that Hickey symbolizes "Mr. O'Neill's subconscious protest against those who have chaperoned and tidied-up his own recent living." No doubt remains that O'Neill was at the end of his emotional tether in 1939. The onset of the war in Europe threw him into a depression from which he never wholly recovered: ideal romantic love failed him, his God remained dead (or died again), and his family past haunted him increasingly. O'Neill admitted as much, and more, himself. In a letter to Lawrence Langner of the Theatre Guild just after finishing *Iceman* he said: "To tell the truth, like anyone else with any imagination, I have been absolutely sunk by this damned world debacle. The Cycle [of plays] is on the shelf, and God knows if I can ever take it up again because I cannot foresee any future in this country or anywhere else to which it could spiritually belong."

O'Neill's biography is crucial, of course, but not in the way it is to *Long Day's Journey*. The latter could not have been written by anyone else, but *Iceman* could. Its affinity to both *The Lower Depths* and *The Wild Duck* has been clearly established. Indeed, it is in some ways easier to relate the literary stream to *Iceman* than it is to relate *Iceman* to O'Neill's own work, particularly his earlier plays. The imminent loss of faith and love, often seen as the same thing, is at the heart of all O'Neill plays, but that link does not tell us why Hickey hated his selfless wife Evelyn enough to kill her, nor why Don Parritt hated his anarchist-mother enough to betray her to the police, nor why Larry Slade hated life enough to become a convert to death. O'Neill went farther into that loss-of-self reality with *Iceman* than he had ever gone before. It leaves us at a loss.

What to do? Freud believed that it is possible for man to live in reality without illusions. With this thought in mind, let us begin with an overlooked statement of the meaning of *Iceman* by—not oddly—a psychiatrist, William V. Silverberg:

> Mankind, [O'Neill] says, is not yet ready for disillusionment; it is very far as yet from being mature enough to be set adrift from its moorings in religion and religion's handmaiden, a coercive morality. And—even more important—whoever attempts in this day and age to emancipate mankind from its illusions with haste, with impatience, with violence, is motivated not by love of man nor by uncompromising devotion to reality, but by hatred and scorn of man, by bitterness, by a sadistic kind of

mischief-making which has as its basis an inability to love any-
body. . . . When men and women have truly learned to love
one another, then they will be mature enough to dispense with
religion and all coercive morality.

If one grants that disillusionment is a necessary stage, then O'Neill's characters are certainly not ready to go. Nor will they be for a long, long time.
They are enchained by the life-destroying haters. And since the pipe dreamers fear death, which is also on the other side of the door of disillusionment,
they shrink away into the pipe dreams at the bottom of the bottle. O'Neill
wants man in reality, but, as Silverberg notes, he disavows hasty, impatient,
and violent emancipators. The two unifying symbols of this destructive
encroachment, as we shall see, are the Anarchist Movement and evangelism.

Harry Hope's bar is the constricted world of total illusion, of life
reduced to nothing. It is a final sanctuary from the busy world of salesmen
and bomb-throwers outside. The "hope" in Harry Hope's name is ironic;
it is the longing for undisturbed somnambulism. The derelicts who nurture
pipe dreams from a rotgut whiskey bottle are not a composite Everyman,
but only a shrinking shadow of Everyman on his fearful journey to death.
Although each derelict has his own escape, together they function as a kind
of Everychorus increasingly throughout the play. Taken together they represent mankind in "the last harbor," or, as Sophus Winther put it, "the
antechamber to the morgue." The derelicts who are on ice are not entirely
dead yet, for they maintain the appearance of life through harmless pipe
dreams about either the past or the future. Until *Long Day's Journey*, a play
in which "the past is the present" and "it's the future, too," O'Neill uses
the past and the future as escape routes from the annihilating present. To
the bums in "Bedrock Bar," the past and the future are interchangeable
havens. Harry Hope, with his rinsed memory of his nagging wife Bessie,
leads the "yesterday movement," while Jimmy Tomorrow leads the "tomorrow movement." "Worst is best here, and East is West, and tomorrow
is yesterday," Larry Slade informs us at the outset of the play.

Into this "End of the Line Cafe" two dormant life forces come to
renew their claims: the Movement and evangelism. Both have been here
before, in the persons of Larry and Hickey, but only for escape. Now they
come for purpose, and it is ironical that they are represented by betrayers;
Hickey has betrayed God's law in killing his wife Evelyn and Don Parritt
has betrayed the Movement in revenging himself against his mother, Rosa.
Both Hickey and Don are too hasty, impatient, and violent. Hickey's effect
on the derelicts and Don's effect on Larry will bear this out.

Sophus Winther is one of the few critics ever to deal with the all-important Movement, and he only briefly. In discussing the barroom bums he says, "Each in his own way was destroyed by his faith in the Cause, the Big Movement, the Ideal of what man should be." It is doubtful that this statement can be made to include all of the derelicts, but, surely, at the deepest level the Movement *does* represent an "Ideal of what man should be," as indeed the real late-nineteenth-century Anarchist Movement did. When Larry Slade, who has retired from the Movement because mankind doesn't want to be saved, learns of the arrest of Rosa and the West Coast anarchists he immediately senses a betrayal, and adds regretfully, "I'd swear there couldn't be a yellow stool pigeon among them" (act 1). Larry is himself an idealist in search of a disillusionment pipe dream, and his high regard for the honesty of the people in the Movement is an outgrowth of that not-dead yearning in him. But Larry is exceptional, as is the offstage Rosa, as was Hugo Kalmar, and—just possibly—Hickey and Don might be. None of the rest of the pipe dreamers possesses enough of a certain something, call it quest, ever to have had faith in a Cause, or to have left it in discouragement. Their spiritual blight came too early in life. To Everychorus, the Movement is irrelevant; they know instinctively that the way to the ideal is through the door of disillusionment, and they fear to go. "I'll make your Movement move!" (act 1) Harry Hope tells Larry in the perfectly disdainful voice of a non-reformer. And Joe Mott, the one-time "white" Negro, senses the underlying violence in the Movement when he says, "If [an anarchist] do ever get a nickel, he blows it on bombs" (act 1).

Hugo Kalmar, the has-been anarchist periodical editor and jail martyr, is a pitifully fascinating example of the Movement's inability to draw the ideal nearer to the real. Hugo loves the proletariat, but he retains the urge to be a God to them, as this typical sample of his drunken musings indicates:

> Hello, leedle peoples! Neffer mind! Soon you vill eat hot dogs beneath the villow trees and trink vine—(Abruptly in a haughty fastidious tone) The champagne vas not properly iced. (With guttural anger) Gottamned liar, Hickey! Does that prove I vant to be aristocrat? I love only the proletariat! I vill lead them! I vill be like a Gott to them! They vill be my slaves! (He stops in bewildered self-amazement).
>
> (act 3)

Hugo suggests the class struggle between the aristocracy and the proletariat, but he is also the tattered remains of the Nietzschean Superman. He lacks Zarathustra's (and Hickey's) "right kind of pity," but he would like to have power anyway. Larry says of Hugo: "No one takes him seriously. That's his epitaph. Not even the comrades any more. If I've been through with the Movement long since, it's been through with him, and, thanks to whiskey, he's the only one doesn't know it" (act 2).

In one way Hugo's plight is the worst of the iced-men, for the magnitude of his crime of aristocratic longings has prevented him from joining either the "tomorrow" or the "yesterday" movement. His past and his future are only rotgut. It is for this reason that he, the nearest to death, is most fearfully aware of death's presence. There are two supreme moments when death is present on the stage in *Iceman,* and Hugo reacts to both of them. When Harry Hope returns from his abortive attempt to take a walk out into the world and finds that, after the horror of reality, his booze no longer has a kick in it, Hugo immediately recognizes that Hope is dead and refuses to sit at his table. At the other moment of death, after Don has leapt from the fire escape, it is Hugo who notices Larry's demise. Once again Hugo refuses to sit at a table of death. "Crazy fool!" he tells Larry in terrified anger. "You vas crazy like Hickey! You give me bad dreams, too" (act 4). To Hugo, Larry's ordering Don out of life is as frightening as Hickey's salvation pitch.

To the Judas of the piece, Don Parritt, the Movement and mother love are one, Rosa Parritt. Don makes this point repeatedly to Larry, the father figure, throughout the play, and Larry does not deny it. "To hear her talk sometimes, you'd think she was the Movement" (act 1), Don tells Larry in act 1. In act 2 he tells him that "She was always getting the Movement mixed up with herself," and in act 3, "The Movement is her life." Don's betrayal of the Movement is the oedipal revenge of a rejected son. As a "free Anarchist," Rosa Parritt was determinedly promiscuous by principle. But Don, like so many other young O'Neill men, cannot reconcile sex and motherhood: whores are defilement and mothers are purity, of that he is certain. Rosa's behavior "made home a lousy place. . . . It was like living in a whorehouse" (act 2). Sharing his reaction with Don is the rejected lover, Larry, who also left Rosa and the Movement, in part, because he did not like living with a whore. It is a great, ironical touch of O'Neill's to have the desperately driven oedipal son come to enlist the father's aid in punishing him for revenging himself against their mutual rival.

Don's life, thus, is finished: for the want of a mother the ideal was lost. Here at this incipient corner of his emotional growth, love failed to enter. And once again the Movement, by sacrificing the one for the many, the short for the long, has spawned violence. By choosing to love all mankind, Rosa has lost the loving of her own son. When Don indicts his mother's hardness of purpose by saying "There's nothing soft or sentimental about Mother" (act 1), he indicts the whole of the grand Anarchist Movement and all such mass nostrums. One can either grow up or grow down, O'Neill says, and this is the way to grow down. Don betrayed his betrayers, Rosa and the Movement, because they acted to unfetter him and leave him alone in the abyss.

The Movement is too humanitarian for Hugo, not humanitarian enough for Don, but too much of both for the Hamlet-like tragic hero of the play, Larry Slade. Early in the play he admits to the contemplative flaw: "I was born condemned to be one of those who has to see all sides of a question. When you're damned like that, the questions multiply for you until in the end it's all question and no answer" (act 1). Larry feels too deeply to act. And because he is a more fully evolved being than most, he is closer to engulfment. His home is the tenuous, shifting no-man's-land between disillusion and nightmare. Objective reality is possible for him, but seemingly too horrible even to consider. Larry's sense of pity derives from his dormant Christianity, while his dejection derives from the failure of the Movement.

At a conscious level, Larry left the Movement, which to him represented mankind's movement toward ideal lifedom, because of his frustration over the slow progress, and because he became aware of the many inevitable pitfalls to which Movers are susceptible. Material greed is the principal one, as it is in all of O'Neill's plays. At the outset of *Iceman,* Larry makes this part of his motives clear: "I'm through with the Movement long since. I saw men didn't want to be saved from themselves, for that would mean they'd have to give up greed, and they'll never pay that price for liberty" (act 1). Just a little later in act 1, Larry tells Don of the pervasive destruction of soul-encroaching greed to mankind as a whole: "The material the free society must be constructed from is men themselves and you can't build a marble temple out of a mixture of mud and manure. When man's soul isn't a sow's ear, it will be time enough to dream of silk purses." That "When," notice, is conditional. It is Larry's (and perhaps O'Neill's) last possible straw to clutch. *When* certain changes have been made in some distant future, man may attain enough fullness of soul to tackle the dilemma of community life. Until then reform is wasted; indeed, Movements are likely to produce more hate than love. Man's loving side, as O'Neill tried to say in *Days without End,* is in constant danger of being overtaken by his hating side.

Without doubt, misdirected love is at the heart of the Movement's dissolution; it can be seen not only in the Rosa-Don betrayals, but just as disastrously in the Rosa-Larry sexual breakup. Rosa's masculine love of freedom destroyed her feminine freedom of love. In this sense, her promiscuity only chained her to a harsh, unwieldy anarchy. Larry, for his part, was not able to absorb the sudden insistence that sexual reform be placed ahead of the love of a man and a woman. Because he thought Rosa put love of mankind above love of man, Larry left her and the Movement. In *Iceman* he still feels the loss of that part of the ideal, as does Rosa, for she still saves his letters. As always, O'Neill makes it clear that the blame belongs to the female. The damage that Rosa does is immense; regeneration is blocked and the future negated. And the loss of love kills Don and half-kills Larry.

The constricting Movement is thus thrice lovelorn: love of friend (Hugo), flesh (Don), and lover (Larry). The loss causes all three to hate: Hugo hates the proletariat, Don hates his mother, and Larry hates himself. All are permanently damaged and inexorably given over to despair. And this major theme of unrecoupable love is echoed throughout the play, as Edwin Engel noticed. To Engel, *Iceman* is O'Neill's unmasking of love:

> Love is an illusion, and all women are bitches or whores. Palpable and undisguised symbols of this truth are the three prostitutes, the only women to appear on the stage. Yet the presence of four others is felt: Hickey's wife, Evelyn; Parritt's mother, Rosa; Hope's wife, Bessie; Jimmie Cameron's wife, Marjorie.

Lack of love, mother love, is the killer of Don; of that we may be certain. But women are not clearly the killers in all of the barroom cases. Jimmy Cameron (Tomorrow), for instance, turned to booze and pipe dreams even before his wife Marjorie began going out with other men. Eventually, Jimmy admits that his wife's adultery was only an excuse: "I discovered early in life that living frightened me when I was sober" (act 3). Inability to go through the door of disillusion is what kills Jimmy and most of the others. Love might sustain one on the way through that abyss, but only possibly. In *Iceman*, we have no successful case. Larry and Rosa's one-time love and Don's and Hickey's ambivalence towards their love objects suggest the possibility, but not the probability. Spiritual strength, soulness, is needed for that. The Movement lacks soul. It symbolizes one of the many means by which modern man, to his great cost, dehumanizes himself.

The Movement, however, is but one-half of modern man's dilemma; his religious failure is the other. The hard-sell evangelism of the Hickeys of the world blights faith just as surely as the Movement blights love. And love and faith are the two prime components of the O'Neill soul. In all his plays the main task is to make these two into one, or, failing this, [to] expose that which prevents the union. It is thus in irony that the Movement is often spoken of as a faith (Hugo "rotted ten years in prison for his faith") (act 2) and Hickey's zeal [is] called a movement ("He's started a movement that'll blow up the world!") (act 2).

Just as Don has absorbed the worst of the Movement, so Hickey has absorbed the worst of religion. The son of a small town Hoosier minister, himself a hardware salesman, Hickey is the false Messiah, as many explicators have pointed out. The pressure of his pitch for a sudden and complete facing up to life only annihilates the feeble pipe dreams by which the "hicks" of mankind live, leaving only the peaceless certainty of death in their place. Motivated by hate, but believing that he is full of love, Hickey brings with him the naked threat of reality. To all those who cannot survive a confrontation with the abyss, and there turn out to be none in *Iceman* who can, the spiritual salesman is the iceman of death. The birthday party that Hickey stages for Harry Hope ironically imitates Leonardo da Vinci's "Last Supper," with Hickey as Christ and the twelve derelicts as his disciples. But the disciples of the self-appointed Christ do not learn faith-love from him; instead, each at his moment of truth turns on Hickey with despair-hate. Throughout the play, it is Hope who most reveals the destructive effects of Hickey's layer-peeling. As Hickey increases the verve of his appeal to him, urging him to take that walk around the ward that he has deferred for twenty years, Hope's good-natured, "without malice" temperament begins to turn into fearful hatred. By the time he actually steps out into the street, he does so "in a sudden fury, his voice trembling with hatred" (act 3). Just as the Movement led to mass violence and hatred, as seen in the bombings on the West Coast, so Hickey's messianic complex led him to kill his wife and to incur the wrath of his fellow man.

In the end, even Hickey senses that his attempt to bring cold-sober reality to Hope's people has been futile. "It was a waste of time coming here" (act 4), he admits to Everychorus just before being led away to prison by Moran (*mors*, death) and Lieb (love). Just before this crushing acknowledgement, Hickey gives up his attempts to convert the men of Hope. In response to the immediate pressure of Hope's exploding resentment, he agrees to put up a "bluff" that he was insane at the time he killed Evelyn and in everything he has said and done in the barroom since. Eric Bentley suggests that the personal love-hate problem between Hickey and Hope is the main cause of Hickey's putting on his "antic disposition," but this must be extended. Hickey never reaches conscious awareness that his evangelism has been wholly destructive; he has not Larry's gift of contemplation. Hickey does *sense*, however, that his own need, and thus mankind's need, for Hope is far more fundamental than his messianic impulse. He sees instinctively that an unconverted Hope, like an uncommitted Don Parritt, is better than a converted and committed hate. Hickey is not able to put his own hate for Evelyn and Hope's hate together, but the audience can. We discover what we knew, that to judge others without having judged ourselves, or without having judged ourselves *accurately,* is both hate-induced and hate-inducing. Hickey can tell us no more, for he cannot take his own death-loving medicine. His only real experience, his hate for Evelyn, was merely an attempt to release his own guilt. Small wonder that, out of charity, he transferred this aim to others, and set out to free all mankind. Like all of the other bums save one, Larry Slade with the intellect, Hickey learns only that pipe dreams must sometimes be replaced, but not pipe dreaming.

Larry Slade is the center balance in the religious theme of *Iceman,* just as he is in the Movement theme. It may be said that he is a deserter of Christianity, but he is not a confirmed one. His progress in the play is from loss of belief to momentary reacceptance to final rejection. Most of the time, as O'Neill's character description of Larry aptly states, "He stares in front of him, an expression of tired tolerance giving his face the quality of a pitying but weary priest's" (act 1). Larry is what O'Neill saw Christianity as being: old, tired, and pitying. But Larry, like modern Western man, cannot help feeling the pull of his Christian heritage, especially when the subject of death is in the air. When Hickey makes a passing jibe at Larry about that "old Big Sleep" during Hope's birthday party, "Larry starts and for a second looks superstitiously frightened" (act 2). At Hickey's announcement of Evelyn's death, Larry again has a "superstitious shrinking" (act 2). And when Larry hears the "crunching thud" of Don's body off the fire escape," "a long-forgotten faith returns to him for a moment" (act 4). Larry's typical superstitious dread is the timeworn product of his residual faith, but his Christ experience at the time of Don's suicide is, as we shall see, a purloined attempt to find Hickey's "right kind of pity."

Self-pity and sometimes pity for others, not Christian compassion, is the non-soulstate to which O'Neill's modern man is reduced. "What pity for oneself and what pity for others?" is, indeed, one wording of the central question in *Iceman.* Instead of the Greeks "Nothing in excess," modern man's motto is "Nothing of pity in excess." All of the characters in *Iceman* have pity problems; it is what unites them. Their degree of forbearance ranges all the way from Don's total self-pity to Evelyn's total selfless pity, with Larry's mixture of pity for himself and others as the standard. Don represents deprivation of love, while Evelyn suggests a surfeit of love. The lovelorn Don grew crooked and, in a moment of hate, betrayed his mother; Evelyn's excess of love caused Hickey to become twisted and, in a similar mood, to kill her. "There's a limit to the guilt you can feel" (act 4), Hickey explains, and he speaks for Don, too, who has also reached this limit. But Don and Evelyn, the two extremes of pity, are also symbolic Christian personages. Don is Judas and Evelyn is the Virgin Mary. Neither sustains life in *Iceman*. Whereas Judas is a negative and Mary a positive force in the Bible, both are negative in *Iceman,* as befits O'Neill's modern world. As Larry puts it, "Honor or dishonor, *faith or treachery* are nothing to me but the opposites of the same stupidity which is ruler and king of life, and in the end they rot into dust in the same grave" (act 2, my italics). Don is not evil and Evelyn is not good; both are merely pitiful. In a sense, Evelyn dies from lack of pity for herself and Don dies for lack of pity for others. The two taken together suggest that pity, to be viable at all, must be balanced between "right" self-pity and "right" pity for others. What is missing in both, of course, is compassion, the willingness to act individually in support of the need to alleviate suffering. As in the other major motifs, this theme of "What price compassion?" is worked out in the tragic hero of *Iceman,* Larry Slade.

Larry is our pity pilgrim, the remnant of Christian man reduced from compassionate commitment to passive pity. Larry pities himself and everyone else, and tries to believe that he is through with active life by assuming the role of "grandstand foolosopher." Until his moment of truth at the end of the play, it is his pipe dream that positive action is not possible in the contemporary world. He retired from the Movement because of the stubborn greed he saw in man and because he lost his faith in love, Rosa. Early in the play, however, it becomes clear that Larry has not lost his humanitarian concern, but that he is in imminent danger of seeing it disintegrate into the distorted, useless self-pity of Hugo. Larry is falling out of life, dying to despair. It is at this point that the revivalist, Hickey, enters.

Hickey, as we eventually learn, by a pipe dream-induced misreading of his own experience completely rejects passive pity and preaches self-help through redemption. He misinterpreted his motive for killing Evelyn. If he *had* done it to "give her peace and free her from the misery of loving" him (act 4) that would have been a loving, mankind-sustaining act. He did not, though. At the taut end of his tethered guilt, he discovered that he hated her. After killing her, as he finally confesses in act 4, he had said, "Well, you know what you can do with your pipe dream now, you damned bitch!" The horror of Hickey's confession lies in his admission that the "not-self" in life can neither be mitigated nor endured, that the infringement of the outer force is both irreconcilable and irreparable. In a sense, one must convert or suffer conversion from others. Hickey chose to become a proselytizer because Evelyn's difference made his loveless self feel guilty. "The sting of conscience teaches one to sting," said O'Neill's preacher, Nietzsche, in *Thus Spake Zarathustra*.

Hickey would rend *some* self-deceit, but not all, and Larry is his one convert. Hickey assigns Larry the task of destroying self-pity (Don). In a key scene between the deluded preacher and the pity pilgrims, Hickey defines his idea of Right Pity:

> Of course, I have pity. But now I've seen the light, it isn't my old kind of pity—the kind yours is. It isn't the kind that lets itself off easy by encouraging some poor guy to go on kidding himself with a life—that kind leaves the poor slob worse off because it makes him feel guiltier than ever—the kind that makes his lying hopes nag at him and reproach him until he's a rotten skunk in his own eyes. I know all about that kind of pity. I've had a bellyful of it in my time, and it's all wrong! (With a salesman's persuasiveness) No, sir. The kind of pity I feel now is after final results that will really save the poor guy, and make him contented with what he is, and quit battling himself, and find peace for the rest of his life.
>
> (act 2)

Although he has not followed this philosophy, Hickey believes what he says, that Right Pity comes from responsible, compassionate action. It is this definition of pity that Larry eventually accepts completely when he acts to order Don out of life. And just as Hickey was wrong in his hate-induced murder of Evelyn, so Larry is similarly wrong in his compulsion for "final results" with Don. The difference between them is the difference between tragedy and pathos—Larry knows it.

From the first, Larry tries to avoid his decision-making responsibility with Don. An act of any kind, he feels, would be regressive; it would return him to a previous, simpler state of existence. It is Larry's illusion that he is out of life by choice, and that to choose to return is both useless and self-destructive. "Look out how you try to taunt me back into life," Larry warns Don. "I might remember the thing they call justice there, and the punishment for—" (act 2). It is precisely this expiation of guilt through punishment that Don wants and that the messianic Hickey wishes to arrange. Don begs for fatherly guidance from both Larry the priest and Larry the sire, and Hickey prods Larry to settle with Don in order to get Larry out of his "grandstand bluff."

Just before the explosion of that pent-up guilt in act 4, however, Hickey's seemingly benevolent motives for dealing with Don turn to hate, just as they had with Evelyn. When Don, the most repugnant character ever created by O'Neill, taunts both Larry and Hickey with the glee of his betrayal of Rosa, Hickey is "disturbed" and says "*with a movement of repulsion:* I wish you'd get rid of that bastard, Larry. I can't have him pretending there's something in common between him and me. It's what's in your heart that counts. There was love in my heart, not hate." Hickey is, of course, self-deluded. There was, and is, hate in his heart, too. Both Hickey and Don suffer from their ambivalence.

In what follows, surely one of the greatest scenes in modern drama, Larry begins by also taking this wrong path towards release. He tries to deal with Don through Hickey's hate. His face is "*convulsed with detestation. His quivering voice has a condemning command in it:* Go! Get the hell out of life, God damn you, before I choke it out of you! Go up—!" Larry is leaving his grandstand, all right, but out of hate. Surprisingly, Don is immediately relieved and immensely grateful to Larry. "I just wanted to be sure," Don says humbly. The irony is that he becomes "sure" by arousing Larry's hate, an emotionally true process that he understands and trusts. Hate itself has its positive side, and not just with Don and Hickey. Larry was impelled by hate, but it led to a compassionate act, and transformed even him, at least momentarily. He now pleads with Don: "Go, for the love of Christ, you mad tortured bastard, for your own sake!" Don answers with awed, pious fumblings to the newly ascended Christ of the piece: "Jesus, Larry, thanks. That's kind. I knew you were the only one who could understand my side of it." For an instant, Larry is Christ, or, as in the Mass, Christ is present in Larry. His kindness is the selfless mercy of Christ, and he is truly the only one who can understand the betrayal of a Judas. Hickey was the false Christ, but here, for this small moment, Larry becomes the true savior. When Don rushes out to jump off the fire escape, it is as a confessed man.

All during Larry's tense wait for the suicide, he wavers between his superstituous dread and his compassion. Hugo observes him and rightly predicts, "Soon comes the Day of Judgment!" When Larry finally hears the sound of Don's body land on the street outside, he says "in a whisper of horrified pity: Poor devil! (*A long-forgotten faith returns to him for a moment and he mumbles*) God rest his soul in peace!" Larry is now at his highest moment of awareness. He has returned to his lost faith, and he can pray for man. But Larry is also at a final point of no return. It is here that he must go over to death or come back to life. It is a problem of emotional choice, not of the will, as it always is in O'Neill's plays. What are the emotional attractions and consequences of an action, any action? And here it should be added that there is no question of whether or not O'Neill introduced "concealed blasphemies in his play" in the Christ symbolism, nor of the possibility that he laughed "in secret at the critics who supposed that he had written a compassionate play in *The Iceman Cometh,*" as Cyrus Day speculated. Larry is truly at his ultimate anguish, and his anguish is that of god-losing modern man, according to O'Neill, caught between Joyce's two worlds.

Immediately after this mystic experience, Larry "opens his eyes" in what is a symbolic awakening and says to himself with the "bitter self-derision" of a totally disillusioned man:

> Ah, the damned pity—the wrong kind, as Hickey said! Be God, there's no hope! I'll never be a success in the grandstand—or anywhere else! Life is too much for me! I'll be a weak fool looking with pity at the two sides of everything till the day I die! (*With an intense bitter sincerity*) May that day come soon! (*He pauses startledly, surprised at himself—then with a sardonic grin*) Be God, I'm the only real convert to death Hickey made here. From the bottom of my coward's heart I mean that now.

Larry is dead, as the final stage direction in the play illustrates; "Larry stares in front of him, oblivious to their racket." In the aftermath of his emotional distillation, he knows that Hickey's "Right Pity" is a failure. His end-stopped past, the Movement and Rosa, had warned Larry against such sudden, violent emancipations, but Hickey's drumming din and Don's piteous plight drew him back to active life. Don's release does not relieve Larry, as he so had hoped; it ends him. Here, at the most nihilistic point in modern drama, Larry yields to the forces of nothingness. The two sides of everything have destroyed him. He can no longer live the lie of a pipe dream of disillusionment, for he knows now that reality is disillusionment. Nor can he live in that reality, for he has only life-denying despair left in him. His "Be God, there's no hope" might well be changed to "*Play* God and there's *still* no hope!" Even when modern man plays God out of love of man, as in Larry's case, he does so only to compensate for his inner ache, his fear of tragic futility, of death. The final irony of Larry's religious failure is that his Christ-act had effect on Don, on betrayal, but not on himself. He is left empty.

Larry's earlier observation, "When man's soul isn't a sow's ear, it will be time enough to dream of silk purses" (act 1), has come home to roost. If Larry is the best of man, a contemplative coward, that still isn't much good. But just as surely, if there is to be a better man, he must come out of Larry. He cannot come from Rosa who now is going to play the "great incorruptible Mother of the Revolution" in prison and say of her son, "I'm glad he's dead!" (act 4). Nor can best man spring from Hickey, the self-proclaimed lunatic. Best man must be nurtured from that still unconquerable part of the Larry Slade who concludes with a "sardonic grin" on his face: "Be God, I'm the only real convert to death Hickey made here." Of such is modern tragedy; not death-defying, but self-defying.

The Door and the Mirror:
The Iceman Cometh

Travis Bogard

O'Neill wrote the first draft of *The Iceman Cometh* between June 8 and November 26, 1939. In this year, the world fell apart as Poland was invaded and Britain and France declared war on Germany. Throughout the end of the Depression, O'Neill had worked on the cycle [of plays, the first called *A Tale of Possessors: The Self-Dispossessed,* the second called *By Way of Obit,* as well as a series of four plays including *The Iceman Cometh, A Moon for the Misbegotten, A Touch of the Poet* and *Long Day's Journey into Night*], finishing drafts of *And Give Me Death, The Greed of the Meek* and *More Stately Mansions.* Work on *The Calms of Capricorn* had begun, but the world crisis made it impossible for him to continue his account of the decline and fall of the United States. In the midst of Armageddon, one does not bother to prophesy. O'Neill's reaction to war was predictable. At Tao House, he retreated further into himself than he had ever gone before, as if the only understanding that could come in a world gone mad was the understanding of one's self. The following year he wrote *Hughie* and the scenarios and some draft versions of its companion works in the cycle of one-act plays called *By Way of Obit.* In 1941, he wrote his last completed work, *A Moon for the Misbegotten.* Although he picked at the [*Possessors*] cycle, making revisions on *A Touch of the Poet* as late as 1942, the work was at a stalemate. Whatever truths it contained for O'Neill had finally to be explored in another past, his own, and in another way than he had in the cycle. The last four plays form a network of introspection whose effect is perhaps best

From *Contour in Time: The Plays of Eugene O'Neill.* © 1972 by Oxford University Press.

49

expressed in O'Neill's words about *The Iceman Cometh* contained in a letter to Lawrence Langner dated August 11, 1940:

> there are moments in it that suddenly strip the secret soul of a man stark naked, not in cruelty or moral superiority, but with an understanding compassion which sees him as a victim of the ironies of life and of himself. Those moments are for me the depth of tragedy, with nothing more that can possibly be said.

Compassion produced by a full understanding of man's circumstances and man's essential nature, a compassion which beggars analysis, is O'Neill's final achievement in theatre. The action of each of the four last plays rests in a tale to be told, a tale that is essentially a confession made in hope of absolution. Although the confessional tale is often plotless, often nothing more than a dream, it is a way of reaching out in the dark, of finding pity long denied to old sorrow.

The introspective qualities of the last plays account for their essential lyricism. When *The Iceman Cometh* was first produced in 1946, under the somewhat ponderously reverential conditions that O'Neill's "return" to the New York theatre necessarily occasioned, it brought with it, from producers and reviewers, charges that O'Neill was indulging himself by refusing to cut the work. Langner tells of a time during rehearsals when he timidly reminded O'Neill that the same point had been made eighteen times. O'Neill told him "in a particularly quiet voice, "I *intended* it to be repeated eighteen times!" Although it was obviously not a matter of calculated intention, O'Neill did not indulge in such repetition without full awareness of its theatrical consequences. Like many of his earlier efforts, the repetition not only in *The Iceman Cometh* but in *A Long Day's Journey into Night* is essential to the lyric mode of the work, for in these plays O'Neill became the poet he had earlier so often lamented he could not be.

Perhaps the nearest theatrical analogue to *The Iceman Cometh* is Dylan Thomas's *Under Milkwood*. Both are "plays for voices," and the voices are those of the dead, reiterating their stories endlessly in an eternity of silence. Under the circumstances of the play the period slang takes on the special qualities of lyric speech. The movement is musical; the repetition of what is said, often almost without significant development, must be followed as if it were music, as patterned abstraction, implemented through contrapuntal repetitions. It is a kind of "sound effect," but here blended so completely with the action that it becomes the action. There are not many moments in theatre comparable to the canonical weaving of the narratives of betrayal, Hickey's and Parritt's, toward the end of the play. Hickey's long monologue is interspersed by short echoing comments from Parritt telling Larry Slade of his own act of betrayal. Parritt and Hickey do not, really, listen to the words that are said. That is to say they do not understand one another and from that understanding receive direction. Rather, they move toward the same end without conscious interawareness, impelled by purely verbal concatenations, each developing the theme of betrayal as a sound in the air. *The Iceman Cometh* does not need music, yet it should be heard as music is heard with an understanding that it progresses in patterns of sound, as much as in patterns of narrative action.

To argue that a play should not be justified by comparison to a musical form has validity. It is, after all, only an analogy, but O'Neill's predilection for Nietzsche would cause him to know that Nietzsche claimed tragedy to have been born from "The Spirit of Music." The lyric movement of the chorus in an Aeschylean or Sophoclean tragedy, *The Coephorii* or *Antigone*, for example, is the source of the play's energy, turning as a massive wheel at the center of the narrative, spinning off the tortured action, and giving it life and form. Similarly, *The Iceman Cometh* has a strong choric thrust, developed in lyric repetitions.

The Iceman Cometh is perhaps the most "Greek" of O'Neill's work, built around a central chorus, complete with *choregos* in Harry Hope, and the three principal actors, Hickey, Slade and Parritt. In creating his chorus, O'Neill turned to his memories of time spent in the saloons of lower New York—Jimmy the Priest's, The Hell Hole, the Golden Swan—and of the people he had met there. Most of the characters are modeled after acquaintances or friends he had observed and whom he placed on stage with special fidelity. Yet while he is concerned to specify their individuality with affectionate concern, he is also seeking, somewhat in the manner of the Elizabethan "Character" writers, to see in the individual a type. The word "type" occurs frequently in his descriptive stage directions of Hope's roomers: Hugo Kalmar bears a "strong resemblance to the type of Anarchist as portrayed . . . in newspaper cartoons"; Joe Mott's face is "mildly negroid in type"; Piet Wetjoen is "A Dutch farmer type." Where the word is not mentioned, the idea remains: James Cameron has "a quality about him of a prim, Victorian old maid." Cecil Lewis "is as obviously English as Yorkshire pudding and just as obviously the former army officer." McGloin has "the occupation of policeman stamped all over him." Ed Mosher "looks like an enlarged, elderly, bald edition of the village fat boy." While the typicality of Willie Oban and of the bartender Rocky is not stressed (although Rocky is summarized as a "Neapolitan-American"), they are not essentially different from the other members of the chorus. The same is true of the three women: Pearl and Margie are called "typical dollar street-walkers," and Chuck Morello, the daytime bartender, like his nighttime counterpart, is seen as an "Italian-American." Harry Hope, the chorus leader, is not viewed as typical in the same way. He maintains a certain individuality partly because it is through him that the liaison is made between the actions of the chorus and the principals. These—Larry Slade, Don Parritt and Theodore Hickman—are individuals, less by their appearance than by the complexity of their emotional problems.

The tableau thus formed, although externally static, has a powerful inner movement. The unity of the chorus is achieved by a remarkable theatrical tour de force. Each of the derelicts has, in the Stanislavskian sense, the same essential action: to foster himself in his dream. The actions create the unity of the microcosm O'Neill has woven. Against its fabric, the protagonists stand sharply drawn. Parritt, Slade and Hickey are seen, perhaps, as aspects of the same man. They overlap at least, in their acts of betrayal, their despairing desire to be rid of pity, their refusal to enter the world of the dreaming chorus. Yet, although they resemble one another, they stand opposed as antagonists as well, forming a hostile triangle against the unity of the background.

The physical picture awakens echoes of other works. O'Neill has evidently had his eye on Gorky's *The Lower Depths,* a play which he appreciated as "the great proletarian revolutionary play," saying that "it is really more wonderful propaganda for the submerged than any other play ever written, simply because it contains no propaganda, but simply shows humanity as it is—truth in terms of human life." The relation between the two works bears analysis, as does the relationship between O'Neill's play and Ibsen's *The Wild Duck,* which like *The Iceman Cometh* explores the fatal effects of the "life-lie." In configuration and *dramatis personae,* Harry Hope's birthday party bears a strong resemblance to the traditional images of "The Last Supper." Such parallels are just and important and in part serve to explain why *The Iceman Cometh* now ranks among the most ambiguous of O'Neill's plays and has received the most extensive critical attention. In its original production, which marked the end of O'Neill's absence from the theatre, and in its 1956 revival in New York, a production that began the resurgence of interest in O'Neill's dramas, it has held a special position in the canon.

Yet viewed in its place in the progress of O'Neill's playwriting career it is not an ambiguous work. In part, it stands as an ironic comment on much that had preceded. Reverting to his earlier manner, spinning an all-but-plotless play filled with portraits of the down-and-out characters he has known as a young man, he recapitulates many of his early themes, particularly that of the "hopeless hope," but removes the romantic coloration with which he clothed the concept in *The Straw*, seeing it now as he was to show it again in *Hughie*, as the only lifeline man could find.

The title, drawn from the story of the wise and foolish virgins in Matt. 25:6, parodies the description of the coming of the Savior: "But at midnight there was a cry made, Behold the bridegroom cometh." The savior who comes to Harry Hope's saloon is a strange messiah. The image of the iceman, suggestive of the chill of the morgue, and of a variety of off-color stories and songs featuring the iceman as a casual seducer, is interpreted by Willie Oban as meaning death: "Would that Hickey or Death would come." Hickey is a messiah of death, but his message, judged by its effect on its hearers, is closely parallel to that of O'Neill's other messiah, Lazarus of Bethany.

O'Neill's two choric dramas, both with titles derived from the New Testament, are at once remarkably like and yet startlingly opposite to one another. In both *The Iceman Cometh* and *Lazarus Laughed,* a messianic figure appears preaching salvation to a world represented in microcosm by type characters. In each play, the recipients of the message prove resistant to it, and when it is forced upon them, prove incapable of acting in accord with it. In each, the messiah is set free to follow his own path to martyrdom by the murder of his wife. That path leads to burning—at the stake and in the electric chair. Such parallels are meaningless except as they relate to the central matter: the messages both messiahs preach, however different in effect and intention, are in essence the same. Of *Lazarus Laughed* O'Neill wrote "Death is the Father, Fear the Holy Spirit, Pain the Son." To this trinity man pays his homage. Lazarus's message to rid men of fear and pain is that they should see life as illusory, give over the dreams that haunt them like ghosts in the dark and acknowledge with clear eyes that they are part of life itself and can ask no higher good. Only then will they know the peace they instinctively seek. Lazarus's doctrine is a lonely one; he loves humanity, but has little room for tenderness and for individual love. Miriam must follow unnoticed behind him, yearning for the simplicity of her life in the hills of Bethany. Those who accept his paradox, that death is life, lose human contact and the powers of sympathy, hope, humility and belief in man. Caught in the Dionysian ecstasy of his laughter, they throw themselves on the swords of soldiers. It is a chill rendition of Matt. 10:39: "He who loses his life for my sake will find it."

Hickey's remedy for the ills of the world, as that world is represented by the types in Harry Hope's back room, is equally cold, equally predicated on a belief that human life is an illusion. As Lazarus exhorts, so Hickey, by means of a series of long, brutal individual encounters in the rooms above the bar, forces the dreamers to give over their ultimate link with life, the sustaining pipe dream of their worth as human beings. Their dreams hold at least an illusion of life's essence: movement in purposive action. Action, to be sure, will never be taken, but the dreams reveal a basic human truth: to foster life, man must preserve a minimal dream of movement. Hickey, whose promised peace is predicated on showing the dreamers that they will never take action and that their dream of doing so is a lie, brings the peace of death. Like much psychiatric theory, Hickey's Godless theology seeks "adjustment" to a meaningless reality, claiming that he who faces his life will find it. Yet if there is no life to be found, Hickey—not unlike Lazarus—becomes Death's priest.

The world which the dreamers inhabit has the fragile ecology of a tide pool. O'Neill calls the saloon "The Bottom of the Sea Rathskeller," and the imagery of drifting tidal life is pervasive. It is a world that barely holds to the fringes of consciousness, moving hesitantly between sleeping and waking, fusing the two conditions into a continuous trance-like existence. The light that filters through the dirty windows from the street is pale and insufficient to separate day from night. Time is meaningless. Voices are nearly unheard in the comatose silence. Existence at Harry Hope's is reduced to its lowest denominator, a hibernation of animals huddled together in dread of waking.

The dreamers have come to Hope's because, ostensibly, they are failures in the outside world, but their typicality makes it impossible to read their communal condition in terms of individual weakness. What lies outside is a world without value, a hostile society to which no man can possibly belong, and from which they must take refuge. At one point, Hickey mocks one of the men, saying, "You can't hang around all day looking as if you were scared the street outside would bite you!" But the menace in the streets is real. The threatening automobile that Harry Hope conjures up to justify his failure to take the walk around the neighborhood is, however imaginary, real. It is a symbol of a mechanized, animalistic, spiritless world, a world in which God is dead.

After the long, poetically oriented quest which he had conducted through the plays of the 1920s, seeking a God to which men could belong, O'Neill at last has come to agree with Nietzsche that men live in a Godless world. There is no longer the possibility of being possessed by Dionysian ecstasy. Men's dreams can have no fulfillment that is not in itself illusion; the mindless, unpoetic materialism of each of the dreams is sufficient testimony to the fact that in all the outer world there is nowhere to go, nothing worth having, nothing to which man may make offering as to a God. In the wake of Hickey's teaching, men are left as walking corpses wandering in an icy hell; all they can do is to wait for death. In *Waiting for Godot,* Samuel Beckett describes the same interminable course of life, as Gogo and Didi indulge in senseless repetitious discourse and vaudeville routines to pass time. The pipe dreams of O'Neill's characters have the same function: they make life tolerable while the dreamers wait for Hickey or Death. As much as each of the dreamers permits himself to understand anything, he knows that the pipe dreams, his own included, are a game, that they are not real. Each man mocks the dreams of the others as insubstantial and illusory, but the mockery is a defensive irony, an essential element of the self-identification the individual's dreams provide. What cannot be admitted is pity, for pity would acknowledge the truth each seeks to conceal from himself. Nietzsche said God died of such pity; in self-pity the lowest creature will come to despair.

For the dreamers, a deliberately fostered illusion is the sign of membership in the club. The subject of the pipe dream is unimportant. Some dreams, like Hugo Kalmar's incoherent anarchist ravings, are little more than fragmented, formless memories, holding so little sense of life as to be meaningless. But whether or not the dream is coherent and contains a goal of action, its value lies less in its shape than in the fact that it forms part of the structure of illusion that "gives life to the whole misbegotten mad lot" of dreamers. The saving possibility is the mutuality of the dreamers' condition, for the conjunction of the dreams, the body heat of sleeping animals, provides the warmth of the world. This fact too makes it possible for the dreamers to hope without desire.

The world in which they live exists beyond desire. Whiskey alone sustains physical life. Hunger for food is not expressed, and notably no movement of sexual desire disturbs the quiet. The three whores arouse no one to lust, nor do they try to become objects of desire among the dreamers. Even the proposed marriage of Chuck and Cora is based on other dreams than that of sexual gratification. Very different from the cycle plays, where sexual battles are fought to the death in an arena of passion, Hope's saloon is a world without women. Nevertheless, as in the cycle plays, the power of woman is felt, and here, too, it is a destructive power.

Hickey's wife, Evelyn, is dead. Rosa Parritt, Don Parritt's mother and Larry Slade's former mistress, has gone to the death of spirit her imprisonment will bring upon her. Yet the power of these women, carried into the dreamers' world by the men who have loved them, destroys for a time the structure of life fostered there. In the cycle plays, Deborah and Sara attempt to use Simon, to destroy his dreams and rid themselves of his desire. Rosa Parritt is pictured as an independent, fierce-willed woman who has held possessively onto her son at the same time as she has refused his love. His claim is that she has forced him into the radical movement, yet has permitted him no freedom of mature judgment. At the same time, he makes clear that he wants her to be his mother and resents her flaunting her lovers in the name of "Free Love." Her lover, Larry Slade, has left her in anger, calling her whore, for much the same reason, so that a bond between Larry and Parritt exists that is like, if it is not in fact, that between father and son, and both feel guilty at having betrayed Rosa in order to be free of her rejection of their love. To love Rosa, a man must submit himself completely to her ambitions, but must make no demands in return. Betrayal is a defensive movement of their individuality.

On the other hand, Hickey's wife has made no ostensible demands on her husband. Hickey's description of her conveys the image of a gentle creature, the opposite of Rosa Parritt, but one who in a different way saps a man's individuality. She asks nothing, fears her husband's attention, yet her capacity for forgiveness, her confident faith in him proves to be as destructive as Rosa's independence. Like Margaret in *The Great God Brown*, Evelyn cannot see what is behind Hickey's face, even when he forces her brutally to look upon it. The blindness of her love makes Hickey live true to her dreams of him and fills him with guilt when he betrays her, just as Parritt and Slade are guilty in their compulsive betrayal of Rosa. O'Neill in the past, sensing that man must belong to some force that controls his being, had shown that those who ran from such possession were in the end caught and destroyed by it. In *The Iceman Cometh,* as in the cycle plays, the force, devoid of its theological implications and reduced to a sexual relationship, has the same effect. Parritt has betrayed his mother to the police, Hickey has murdered Evelyn, and Larry must send his "son" to his death to end his torment, resigning himself finally to the sort of living punishment that Lavinia Mannon accepts. Each seeks death as the only way of assuaging or atoning for the guilt the woman has thrust upon him. Had Simon survived his final rejection by Deborah, something of the same death-leaning emptiness might well have overtaken him.

The three betrayers are the only occupants of the saloon who need pity. They epitomize, perhaps, the men without dreams who live in the hostile streets beyond the barroom door. They come, at least, from such a world, and disturb the dreaming sea. Both Hickey and Parritt force pity into the waters, but it is pity without tenderness. Parritt demands that Slade take pity on him and punish him by commanding him to suicide. Hickey, who insists that Larry's instinctive sympathy for the dreamers is the wrong kind of pity, attempts to rip off their masks and free them of the torture of hope. The play charts his failure and notes as well the way returning illusion brings life again to the sterile waters. When he has gone, old currents move again at the bottom of the sea, and the men who have been awakened to a hideous and intolerable truth begin to dream again.

Hickey's therapy, through different means, is worked on Cornelius Melody [in *A Touch of the Poet*]. When his role as the romantic soldier is taken from him, he like the bums becomes a comatose, dying animal. He saves himself by assuming another role, as the bums reclothe themselves in illusions. Deborah Harford, too, enters a world like Hope's saloon when she enters the summer house at the end of *More Stately Mansions*, but she must live alone, in the isolation of insanity. Deborah's end is so dark as to be indiscernible.

The Iceman Cometh, however, is illuminated by "darkness visible," and it reflects the despair O'Neill himself felt in the year of its composition. On September 11, 1939, he wrote to Langner from Tao House,

> The whole business from 1918 to now has been so criminally, hoggishly stupid. That is what sticks in one's gorge, that man can never learn but must be always the same old God damned greedy, murderous, suicidal ass! I foresee a world in which any lover of liberty will continue to live with reluctance and be relieved to die.

That it would be a relief to die! The desire that surges to the surface of the lives of the three betrayers in the play was a common reaction in that year. O'Neill was not alone.

The Late Plays and the Development of "Significant Form": *The Iceman Cometh*

Jean Chothia

In 1933 O'Neill withdrew completely from public life and from active participation in the theatre in order to concentrate on his writing. Between 1933 and 1939, he was involved in an increasingly frustrating struggle with his projected cycle of plays, which were to deal with the private and public lives of an American family from the Revolution to the 1930s. By the end of 1943, his physical health was breaking down, and his slowly worsening palsy was to prevent him from writing during the remaining ten years of his life. But in 1939 he set aside the cycle and within four years had written the five plays which I have called "the late plays." Although he held these plays back from production there is a note of confidence and excitement when he mentions them in letters. This is particularly true of *The Iceman Cometh* and *Long Day's Journey into Night* which he said he had "wanted to write for a long time." He wrote to Barrett Clark in 1943:

> Although I have done no writing lately, my record since Pearl Harbor is not as poor as it might be. I have finished, except for a final cutting, another non-Cycle play—"A Moon For the Misbegotten"—and rewritten the 1828 Cycle play "A Touch of the Poet," done some work off and on on another non-Cycle "The Last Conquest"—anti-totalitarian state, anti-Instrumentalist philosophy, but useless as present war propaganda because it is a symbolic fantasy of the future, and of the last campaign for the

From *Forging a Language: A Study of the Plays of Eugene O'Neill.* © 1979 by Cambridge University Press.

59

final destruction of the spirit—which (happy ending!) does not succeed.

When, in addition, I consider "The Iceman Cometh," most of which was written after war started in '39 and "Long Day's Journey Into Night," written the following year—(these two plays give me greater satisfaction than any other two I've ever done)—and a one act play "Hughie," one of a series of eight I want to do under the general title, "By way of Obit," I feel I've done pretty well in the four war years.

The Last Conquest never was written and the scenario and notes which survive are not at present available to scholars. The other five plays, as O'Neill suspected, and as I have already suggested in references to them [elsewhere], represent a different kind of achievement from his previous work.

Early in his career, as I showed [elsewhere], O'Neill had realized that the "ruthless selection and deletion and concentration on the emotional—the forcing of significant form on experience" were "the task" of the writer. Given such early recognition of the necessity of ordered form, why should O'Neill's writing have achieved "crisis and consistency" only between 1939 and 1943? Did his new certainty of dramatic form allow him to focus his experience more sharply, or did the pressure of subject matter create the necessary formal rigour? These two questions can probably not be answered adequately even in the most probing biography. All we can do is note factors which may be relevant. We know that O'Neill's isolation allowed him to concentrate on his writing and set it apart from the twenty years of experimentation, to which he could, therefore, look back as to an apprenticeship during which he had stretched and tried his medium until he knew it thoroughly. We can guess that his isolation must also have given him time and space in which to confront his own past and measure his present against his adolescent self. And certainly, his letters show that events in Nazi Germany and the outbreak of war in Europe had shaken him deeply, and that he sensed there was not much writing time left to him. But these cannot be more than suggestions. A study such as I have undertaken cannot explain a sudden burst of creative imagination. It *can* explore what resulted from it.

What has emerged most forcibly for me from reading and seeing performances of the late plays is exactly this, that in each of them we feel the presence of a creative imagination, shaping and controlling the elements of the play. Nothing is arbitrary or unfinished as it so often was in the past.

The material, drawn from the period of O'Neill's late adolescence, is openly autobiographical, but it is treated with an objectivity which was lacking when similar material was only latent in plot and characterization in the earlier work. The emphasis in my discussion will be different from that in the earlier chapters [of *Forging a Language*]. There, I suggested that whilst the plays written before 1934 did have intrinsic interest, their significance lay in what their inventiveness and seriousness contributed to the American theatre and in how their themes and methods prefigured those of the late plays. I made general points and illustrated them from particular plays. Now the commentary on individual plays will be central: the language of *The Iceman Cometh,* first, and then *Long Day's Journey into Night* [not discussed here], will be examined in detail.

The variety of language in the late plays and the appropriateness of speech to speaker is striking, particularly in contrast to the monotony of the middle plays. O'Neill now draws on a wide range of dialects and idiolects and juxtaposes standard English with low-colloquial. "Talk" is no longer a "straitjacket" and dialect no longer a "dodge," because both are used and neither is an end in itself.

In my consideration of *The Iceman Cometh,* I shall be more concerned with broad discussion of how elements are patterned and, [elsewhere] in that of *Long Day's Journey into Night,* there will be more close analysis. It is rewarding to vary the method in this way, because the language of the two plays is organized somewhat differently. Both plays stir wonder and despair about the human condition, both portray the peculiar persistence with which men patch up their lives and go on living against all odds, but these important similarities have blurred recognition of the formal differences between the two plays and of the differing areas of human experience which they explore. The two plays are not alike: they are complementary.

The dramatic effect of *The Iceman Cometh* derives, firstly, from the success with which O'Neill differentiates all seventeen characters who people Hope's bar and makes us interested in them, so that the stage seems to teem with life and, secondly, from the way in which he varies and interweaves their words so that the activity of each at any given point, besides characterizing that figure, contributes to the ongoing action of the play. The effect derives, also, from the fact that one character is treated more fully than the rest and so stands in a different relation to the audience from the other figures and helps to shape their response to the action. I shall, therefore, examine the verbal basis for the differentiation of the seventeen and of their interweaving and will look at the characterization of the differently focused figure, Larry Slade. In *Long Day's Journey into Night,* there are four central characters, all of whom are at least as fully developed as Larry Slade is. The language does differentiate them from each other, but it also reveals each as being many-faceted and divided against himself. As the play progresses and we seem to know each more fully, the differences between the characters come to seem less significant than the human existence they share. . . .

At the opening of *The Iceman Cometh,* all except two of the characters on stage are asleep and most will remain so for three-quarters of the very long first act, only occasionally surfacing from their slumber. There will be very little movement about the stage. Indeed, during the rest of the play, most of the characters will be seated. This physical stillness establishes the mood of inertia which characterizes the "last harbour" where no one worries "where they're going next, because there is no further they can go." It is a daring device, particularly for a writer who has produced plays as monotonous as *Lazarus Laughed* and *Mourning Becomes Electra.* An account of why it succeeds would amount to a description of the changes that have taken place in O'Neill's control over form since he wrote the middle plays. Movement and gesture, for instance, are far more effectively, if less histrionically, used than then. What physical action there is in this generally static play comes at vital moments and makes these more striking precisely because of the contrast with the usual physical stillness. Every character on stage, for example, rouses himself, loses his slouching posture and listens alertly in response to the news that Hickey has been sighted. The concerted movement reinforces the impression we have already gained from the dialogue of the eager anticipation of Hickey's arrival by all the roomers. The greater subtlety now in the handling of movement is matched by the dynamism of the dialogue. The dialogue here entertains the audience, offers them information which augments what they already know or makes them reassess what they thought they knew, and continually stimulates them to make connections. O'Neill's carefully balanced distribution of the dialogue amongst the characters ensures that the audience's attention is continually shifted from one to another of them.

In the opening exchange of the play, O'Neill is already offering visual and oral information, posing questions, raising doubts. When the play begins, a large number of obviously down-at-heel men are asleep around the tables of a dingy bar. Two characters are awake. One is sitting at the extreme left front of the stage. The other passes him a bottle:

ROCKY (*in a low voice out of the side of his mouth*). Make it fast.
(*Larry pours a drink and gulps it down. Rocky takes the bottle and*

puts it on the table where Willie Oban is.) Don't want de
boss to get wise when he's got one of his tightwad buns
on. (*He chuckles with an amused glance at Hope.*) Jees, ain't
de old bastard a riot when he starts dat bull about turnin'
over a new leaf? "Not a damned drink on de house," he
tells me, "and all dese bums got to pay up deir room
rent. Beginnin' tomorrow," he says. Jees, yuh'd tink he
meant it. (*He sits down on the chair at Larry's left.*)

LARRY (*grinning*). I'll be glad to pay up—tomorrow. And I
know my fellow inmates will promise the same. They've
all a touching credulity concerning tomorrows. (*A half-
drunken mockery in his eyes.*) It'll be a great day for them,
tomorrow—the Feast of All Fools with brass bands
playing! Their ships will come in loaded to the gunwales
with cancelled regrets and promises fulfilled and clean
slates and new leases!

ROCKY (*cynically*). Yeah, and a ton of hop!

LARRY (*leans toward him, a comical intensity in his low voice*).
Don't mock the faith! Have you no respect for religion,
you unregenerate Wop? What's it matter if the truth is
that their favouring breeze has the stink of nickel whiskey
on its breath and their sea is a growler of lager and ale,
and their ships are long since looted and scuttled and
sunk on the bottom? To hell with the truth! As the
history of the world proves, the truth has no bearing on
anything. It's irrelevant and immaterial as the lawyers
say. The lie of a pipe dream is what gives life to the
whole misbegotten mad lot of us, drunk or sober. And
that's enough philosophic wisdom to give you for one
drink of rot-gut.

ROCKY (*grins kiddingly*). De old Foolosopher, like Hickey calls
yuh, ain't yuh? I s'pose you don't fall for no pipe dream.

The first speaker's words are supported by gesture until we are accustomed
to his vernacular. What he says and how he says it indicate his occupation,
his social class, and his regional base, tell us where the action takes place,
and prepare us, by gesture and through an imitation, to hear the voice of
one of the sleeping figures whilst, at the same time, warning us not to
believe all we hear. When the second man speaks, we recognize that there
is understanding between them. There are some phrases in Larry's speech

which echo Rocky's New York City slang, and Larry actually takes over the word "tomorrow" and uses it with reference to himself and then repeats it twice more, echoing Rocky's warning and extending it to include everyone on the stage. There is continuity between the words of the two speakers, therefore, but there is also a startling linguistic contrast. Apart from the slang phrases, Larry speaks Standard English and uses vocabulary which marks him (despite the obvious poverty of his dress) as of a different social class and educational background from his interlocutor. The pace of his speech is different: unlike Rocky's, all his verbs have subjects, which slows his speech slightly, as does the length and archaic flavour of some of his words, such as "touching credulity," "gunwales," "favouring breeze." But the contrast goes further than this, and the structure of the speech governs the kind of delivery each actor must adopt. Rocky's speech is crude and terse, Larry's reveals him to be a man who enjoys words, who plays with them, creating pictures, whose way of thinking is reflected in his fluency. His thought is elaborated by verbal devices, by hyperbole, alliteration (most frequently on the *l*s), and symmetry of phrasing (in the phrase "cancelled regrets and promises fulfilled," with its past participle + plural noun, plural noun + past participle and its assonance in the repeated -*lled* ending, for example). One image, the "Feast of All Fools" seems, by a reference to the traditional motif of the ship of fools, to suggest the succeeding one, as Larry spins out his description of the roomers' dreams. The growing length of the sentences also suggests that an idea is being elaborated. But when his subject seems to change in the next utterance and he describes the reality, his tone does not: he uses an even longer sentence (forty-six words) and an anticlimactic reflection of the same image, in which the feast is cheap alcohol and the ships, with an alliterative flourish, as "long since looted and scuttled and sunk."

If the verbal display does not yet, in this first exchange, raise uncertainties about how seriously Larry's philosophy is to be taken, it does indicate that there is some showmanship in him, particularly when it is punctuated by Rocky's cynical interjections, "de old Foolosopher, ain't yuh?" and, soon "de old anarchist wise guy dat knows all de answers!" The differences between the speech of the two men help us to perceive each more clearly, and yet the evidence that they converse easily despite those differences is the first signal of how integrated the community in Hope's bar is. Virtually none of this information is stated in so many words by the characters. It is absorbed by the audience from the very shape and organization of the dialogue. Clearly, any one auditor will not register all these points and he will probably register others which I have not mentioned, but he will be aware that the dialogue has a dense texture and that the more fully he concentrates on it, the more he will glean, which creates a state of receptivity in the audience from the outset of the play. O'Neill is ensuring, therefore, in the opening words a degree of engagement by the audience which he achieved only in the final scene of *Mourning Becomes Electra*.

In his one-act sea plays, O'Neill used a variety of regional dialects to differentiate his characters and to create an interesting surface texture. As the contrast between the speech modes of Rocky and Larry has indicated, O'Neill returns to this method in *The Iceman Cometh*, although now the variation is more complex and the information it provides more extensive. O'Neill's success in the sea plays depended on each accent being immediately recognizable and being quickly succeeded by a quite different one. The differentiation was bold, if not crude, and each character was derived from the stereotype traditionally associated with the national dialect he used. The variation amongst those sunk to the bottom in Hope's bar is wider than it was on the S.S. *Glencairn*. If those plays offered a shadowy image of America, as I suggested [elsewhere], the image presented here is much more clearly focused.

The speech of thirteen of the characters in *The Iceman Cometh* is individualized, lexically and syntactically. The speech of four more, the tarts and second bartender, is similar to that of Rocky, with whom they form a subgroup among the characters. They have a particular role in the action which will be discussed later. The land, the law, the army, local and national politics, journalism and entertainment are represented here. There are men of various ages and men who are aware of having been sons, husbands, lovers. Not only nationality but class, education and, therefore, degrees of articulacy are communicated through speech. Four characters, Larry (Irish), Jimmy (Scottish), Lewis (English) and Oban (American, upper class), speak Standard English with a slight colouring of national accent, and are able to use a variety of syntactic transformations. The speech of Hickey and Parritt is American Standard with occasional colloquial solecisms. Their sentences are usually simple, sometimes compound. That English is the second language of two, Hugo (Central European) and Piet (Afrikaans), is indicated by pronunciation through vowel and consonant shifts (Hugo: "leetle," "vill," "trink"; Piet: "plind," "chentleman," "dot" [that]), by occasional confusion between singular and plural forms, and by irregular word order ("Always there is blood . . . "; "Vit mine rifle I shoot damn fool Limey officers py the dozen, but him I miss."). The remaining characters speak New York low-colloquial, but amongst them, too, social degrees are apparent. Harry, Mosher and Mcgloin use a great deal of slang vocabulary, and Mcgloin has occasional Irish markers, but low-colloquial syntax and phonology is only present in the speech of Rocky's group and of Joe, who also has some specific markers of low-colloquial negro speech. These are much the same as O'Neill developed in presenting New York low-colloquial in the early plays ("boin" [burn], "t'ink" [think], "dese" [these], "yuh" [you]. "Was" generally replaces "were" and terminal "*g*s" are dropped. "Git" [get], and "does you?," "is you?" and "you better" are used by Joe).

O'Neill composes an idiolect for each man by combining regional dialect with occupational dialect. The argot of each man's abandoned occupation intrudes into his speech. It reveals his past but also shows that each man's past still possesses him: his very thought is shaped by the language he retains. We can identify in Hope's bar a one-time confidence trickster ("rube," "short-change"), a policeman ("fine pickings," "sugar galore"), a gambler ("play craps," "my stake") and amongst the middle-class characters, an anarchist ("Bakunin's ghost," "Hickey the Nihilist"), a journalist ("bitter sorrows," "losing the woman one loves by the hand of death"), a college student (Willie retains both student slang, "the rah, rah boys," and student humour, as when he ascribes his bawdy song to Emerson or Jonathan Edwards) and, with Hickey's arrival, a salesman ("honesty is the best policy," "Now listen, boys and girls, don't look at me as if I was trying to sell you a gold brick. Nothing up my sleeve.").

Dion Boucicault introduced a "melting pot" cast into his melodrama, *The Octoroon* (1859). The outline given here of the range achieved by O'Neill shows it to be much subtler than Boucicault's but does not reveal how much more functional it is; for that, the organization of the speech of a few of the characters must be examined in greater detail. I cannot deal with all of them, but my discussion of the way O'Neill handles the speech of these few will serve as a model of what he does with the rest. The individual strands which will be separated here are closely interwoven in the play. The speech of Rocky's group will be examined first and then that of Harry Hope, of Captain Lewis and of Hugo.

Rocky and his group use a large number of slang words. Many of them are variant forms of address. The "tarts" are also "pigs," "hookers," "hustlers," "tramps," and "your stable"; a man is a "dope," a "poor sap," a "louse," a "sucker," a "bastard," a "boob from de sticks." Cora's face is "a clock"; the party, "dis boithday racket"; the bar, "dis dump." What is most noticeable is the undertone of abuse, even when none is intended by the speaker. It is exaggerated by the rhetorical way they phrase their questions with a terse "ain't yuh?," "dat's you, huh?" and by the violence of their threats: "I'd like an excuse to give you a good punch in the snoot," "If yuh opened your yap, I'd knock the stuffin' outa yuh," "I'd . . . mop up de street wid him."

In an attack on Mencken's praise of American slang, Marius Bewley described such elements and said of them: "Their intention is nothing less than degradation, for they have their origin in an ancient sense of inferiority (and perhaps guilt) seeking to escape from itself through brutality." The slang of Rocky's group is, in the first place, suggestive of the limited opportunity of their lives. The roomers have finally fallen to Hope's bar; Rocky and his group begin there. There is social comment as well as comic irony in the fact that their status-illusion is based on semantics and that they recognize fine degrees in their abusiveness: they are "tarts," not "whores"; "bartenders," not "pimps." O'Neill emphasized the difference by cutting out phrases like "a lot of crap," "shut your trap" from the speech of the roomers in the final draft of the play. There is no real crudity or physical unpleasantness in the play. O'Neill made no use of the choking "lungers" and freely used spittoons that biographers describe as being commonplace in the bars on which Hope's is modelled, nor does he use obscene language. The language of Rocky's group provides the feeling without any of the distracting horror. Similarly, in the preface to *Oliver Twist*, Dickens comments on his having modified the language of Sykes to give the true flavour whilst avoiding particularly offensive elements.

It has other functions, too. Rocky's group exists partly in Hope's bar and partly in the outside world. Rocky rushes between the public bar and the inner room, the girls burst in from the street, laughing and banging doors. They set the play in relation to external time and society. Because O'Neill shows the outside world through their eyes, a world of "saps" in which men prey on each other, the harmony and mutual support of the life in Hope's bar is made more valuable and the collapse of that society, when its members confront the world, more grievous. The roomers, too, become abusive and even physically violent towards each other, under pressure of their meeting with the world. At the end of the play, O'Neill keeps Pearl and Margie off stage until after the departure of Hickey. Their harsh voices, as they crash drunkenly on to the stage describing themselves at last as "whores," come as a reminder to the audience of the outside world which has finally been rejected by the roomers. The lateness of their entrance allows O'Neill to use the visual image of the door being closed on that world.

I mentioned, in my discussion of the opening exchange, the contrast between the speed of Larry's and of Rocky's utterance. Much of the plot is relayed in the exchanges between members of Rocky's group which begin each act. It is relayed economically because they talk faster and more tersely than the other characters. In the final draft of the play, O'Neill cut short some of their speeches to obtain a better dovetailing effect. In the first typescript, for example, Pearl says "nobody can't call me a whore" (act 2). In the final text, this becomes:

> PEARL. Nobody can't call me a —
> ROCKY. Aw, bury it! What are you, a voigin?

Even sentimentality hardly drags when it is as much to the point as:

> ROCKY. You're aces wid me, see?
> PEARL. You're aces wid us too. Ain't he, Margie?
> MARGIE. Sure, he's aces.

The cynical name-calling of this group helps to remind the audience of the self-deceptions the roomers are practising, and their questioning keeps the audience alert. Rocky establishes doubt about Parritt, for example, before this character appears because of his insistent questions: "Who's de new guy? . . . Why ain't he out dere sticking by her? . . . But what kind of sap is he to hang onto his right name?"

But if O'Neill saw what Bewley saw in American slang, he knew as Mencken claimed, that at its best it contained "pungent humour and bold- ness of conceit," and uses this element, too. In the early plays, O'Neill deliberately limited his use of slang and other forms of low-colloquial in order to project, through their very groping for language, the emotional inarticulacy of his characters. Their vernacular had to be remote from the robust, inventive American speech praised by Whitman and Twain. Now O'Neill can allow his characters to "spread themselves." There is a good deal of colourful slang: champagne is that "old bubbly water" and we hear of "a case of almost fatal teetotalism." But Harry Hope, the man "whom every one likes on sight" (stage directions), whom we see acting as the benefactor of all the roomers, appropriately has the fullest command of Mencken's kind of slang.

Harry's language draws the audience's affection to him because it is so entertaining. We enjoy listening to him talk. He uses fantastic inventions and farfetched images, in telling of how the bums give him the "graveyard fantods" or recalling a time when his wife was so annoyed "she coulda bit a piece out of the stove lid." His use of hyperbole takes the edge off his threats and complaints and gives credence to Rocky's opening comment on him, "Jees, you'd t'ink he meant it." It also helps to convey the barroom mood to the audience as do the yarns the roomers spin and the jokes they tell. This is Harry:

> You and Chuck laughing behind my back, telling people you throw the money up in the air and whatever sticks to the ceiling is my share.

> There ain't going to be no more drinks on the house till hell freezes over.

> If there was a war and you was in it, they'd have to padlock the pockets of the dead.

The kind of inventiveness involved here is often compared by the commentators on American slang with poetic metaphor. I think that these examples show that the two are different largely because their function is so different. The slang phrase is delightful in itself. It draws attention away from whatever is being discussed to its own ingenuity or comic hyperbole. It decorates speech rather than illuminates it, while poetic metaphor takes the reader or auditor inwards into the meaning of the utterance, and is most fully alive in the context for which it was coined. The value of the slang phrase lies in its capacity to be absorbed into the communal vocabulary. Its effective life is limited because repeated usage will gradually dull the pleasure it gives. O'Neill avoids this problem of dulling by using, quite appropriately since the play is set in 1912, slang which is no longer in common usage and so will not be blunted by being well-known to the audience. I have cross-checked O'Neill's slang against several collections of American slang and, interestingly enough, found that virtually all the lexical items he uses were authentic and are recorded in one or another of the dictionaries. This includes some of the particularly appropriate epithets, which one might have imagined were coined by O'Neill: (Weseen, *Dictionary of American Slang*) "foolosopher," an expression that Professor M. C. Bradbrook tells me was current in Elizabethan English, "Harp" [Irishman], "rah, rah boys." But whether it is invented or remembered, O'Neill's slang *seems* authentic because of the use of hyperbole and of ingenious elaboration.

O'Neill utilizes the affection Harry's speech rouses in the audience to bind them emotionally later in the play. When Harry returns, the first to have failed Hickey's challenge, he is badly shaken so that even Hickey admits "I didn't think he'd be hit so hard. He's always been a happy-go-lucky slob." Harry's language reinforces this testimony. O'Neill makes his words harsh and crude, "Bejees, you're a worse gabber than that nagging bitch, Bessie was" and then lets his language shrink into terse sentences of mono-syllabic words, "I want to get drunk and pass out. Let's all pass out. Who the hell cares?" It is the degraded aspect of American slang which is now apparent in his speech, reflecting his mental state. The audience listens as eagerly as the roomers when, after Hickey's departure, Harry reverts to his earlier robust way of expressing himself. The spiritual resurgence is clearly displayed in the linguistic resurgence. The speech which initiates the change is a remarkable one. It is rhythmically patterned: a personal cry, beginning with his habitual oath, "Bejees," and the first-person pronoun, alternates with a general statement about Hickey's mission which begins with the third-person pronoun, "it":

> *Bejees,* fellers, *I'm* feeling the old kick, or *I'm* a liar! *It's* putting life back in me! *Bejees,* if all *I've* lapped up begins to hit me, *I'll* be paralysed before I know it! *It* was Hickey kept me from—. *Bejees, I* know that sounds crazy, but he was crazy, and he'd got all of us as bughouse as he was. *Bejees, it* does queer things to you having to listen day and night to a lunatic's pipe dreams . . . (my italics).

He is almost singing when he reaches the climax,

> Bejees, it's good to hear someone laugh again! All the time that bas—poor old Hickey was here, I didn't have the heart—Bejees, I'm getting drunk and glad of it! (*He cackles and reaches for the bottle.*) Come on fellers. It's on the house.

Harry seems to lead the others back to life with this joyful paean. The emotional response of the audience derives less from the paraphraseable meaning of the utterance than from its rhythmic and syntactic structure and from its relationship to all Harry's preceding utterances.

But the roles of Rocky and Harry Hope are central in the play and it might be expected that the dramatist would pay particular attention to their speech. We will see, when we turn to the two minor roles, that each character is fully integrated into the action. We have the impression that Hope's bar is peopled with all sorts and conditions of men because each is etched sharply, and, in every case, the speech is the man. Among the notes for the play there are detailed descriptions of all the characters. How clearly O'Neill heard each from the outset is evident in the scenario, which consists of snatches of what will become characteristic dialogue, joined by a running commentary; how clearly he saw each character is evident in the detailed descriptions in the introductory stage directions. At every turn of the action, we hear every man's voice, even if, in the interests of economy, the voice is sometimes limited to a single utterance. This brings a feeling of multiplicity to the play such as O'Neill intended in *Lazarus Laughed* but failed to achieve despite the complicated mask scheme. The difference between the two plays reveals how necessary that early dictum of O'Neill's, "Life in terms of lives," was to his particular kind of dramatic imagination. The way in which O'Neill makes time for every voice to be heard in this play makes a claim for the individual value of every man, and is one of the major positive statements of the play. In *Death of a Salesman,* Miller tells us that "attention must be paid" to Willy Loman. O'Neill has no need for such didactic commentary. The very presence of each character is a demand for attention.

O'Neill's portrayal of Captain Lewis comes closest to using a national stereotype. Lewis's command of syntax tells us that he is educated, and his articulacy is emphasized because we usually hear him in conversation with Wetjoen, whose English is halting and heavily accented. That he is English is established by his use of characteristic epithets, "my dear fellow," "old chum," "the only bloody sensible medico," and by a certain pomposity of phrasing, "my *profound* apologies," and of attitude: this destitute man will save for a *first*-class passage home and will accept any job however humble, but "not *manual* labour, *naturally*." The jauntiness of the ex-army officer is marked by the occasional use of "what?" as a rhetorical coda at the end of sentences and by the liberal use of "bloody." But O'Neill also plays with the stereotype to make the character more complex. Lewis gives his word "as an officer and a gentleman" when he clearly has no intention of keeping it. The stiffness associated with the British in America is reflected in the pedantry of Lewis's speech, but the pedantry is, in its turn, often the source of deliberate humour on Lewis's part, as when he avoids discussion of an outstanding debt with the words, "Sorry. Adding has always baffled me. Subtraction is my forte." Our appreciation of the humbug underlying this kind of humour is reinforced by the information that Lewis came to America to work in the Boer War spectacle at the St Louis Fair, so that it is with a delighted recognition of the inevitable that we discover that, just as the boasts of great strength of his sparring partner, Wetjoen, are belied by what we see of his physical weakness, so Lewis, too, has betrayed his stereotype by having embezzled regimental money.

The presence of Lewis, like that of every character, contributes to the central action. Specifically, it does so through his seemingly inconsequential description of his friend as "my balmy Boer who walks like a man" which is followed by a joke in which he compares Wetjoen to a baboon. The response of the other characters implies that this is a habitual joke, and this impression is reinforced when the joke is repeated in act 3 and the pun laboured by being explained. When the joke is told a third time, after Harry's paean, the repetition of the familiar acts as a signal to the audience that the roomers are following Harry's lead and are beginning to reconstruct their former life style.

We are constantly aware of Lewis, although his is one of the smallest roles in the play. His physical presence sketched in some detail by O'Neill in the stage directions is as striking as his words—he is tall and erect, is bewhiskered and frequently strips off his shirt to reveal a ragged scar. Every other character is intended to be equally distinct visually. The description given here of Lewis together with what we have seen of the pattern of his speech indicates O'Neill's method in the play. The figures are not fully rounded as we shall see [elsewhere] those in *Long Day's Journey into Night* are, but nor are they simply types or humours. In each case, O'Neill sketches the outline of a whole man, and adds to this a few telling details. By developing and rearranging these details, he projects the character. This is the art of the caricaturist. O'Neill is adopting the method used by Dickens when he depicts figures like Micawber or Betsy Trotwood and the figures in Hope's bar have comparable clarity. They are memorable in a way that more fully drawn characters could not be and, because we can therefore hold them in our minds simultaneously, O'Neill is able to interweave them to form the patterned action. The discovery by O'Neill's biographers of prototypes for each of the roomers in Hope's bar reinforces rather than contradicts this point. O'Neill himself wrote:

> The dump in the play is no one place, but a combination of three in which I once hung out. The characters all derive from actual people I have known—more or less closely or remotely—but none of them is an exact portrait of anyone.
> (To Macgowan, November 29, 1940)

Doris Alexander's detailed description of Hyppolyte Havel, for example, demonstrates convincingly that Hugo is derived from him. But to show that O'Neill worked from life is not to prove that he recreated that particular life on the stage, and to suggest that he did is to miss what he is actually doing. The caricaturist, too, works from life.

Hugo is described by O'Neill as having the appearance of "the type of anarchist as portrayed bomb-in-hand in newspaper cartoons." His speech and action are more restricted than those of any other figure on the stage. His appearance is bizarre and so is his manner of suddenly waking from sleep to cry the revolution before sleeping again. He speaks almost entirely in two- to six-word exclamations, made more elliptical by his foreign syntax and pronunciation and by his frequent use of revolutionary jargon: "Capitalist svine! Bourgeois stool pigeon! Have the slaves no right to sleep even?" This first utterance of his is typical, and conveys the extent to which he has atrophied in Hope's bar. It is reminiscent of the speech of the revolutionary socialist, Long, in *The Hairy Ape* but, as the play progresses we see how differently it is handled. We find that, whilst the shape of the utterances continues to suggest Hugo's sterility, O'Neill rearranges the content making it surprisingly expressive both of the Hugo that once was and of the Hugo who, for all his atrophy, still has the remnants of human emotions, still feels panic and fear and still needs to maintain some kind of belief in himself. After Hickey has quietly pointed out that Hugo's anger when the champagne is not properly iced is incongruous with the revolutionary ideals he boasts, O'Neill endorses Hickey's point and, suggesting Hugo's panic, gives an impression of unconscious thought welling into speech, because he includes in Hugo's outburst a succession of self-condemning oppositions and incongruities, "I love only the proletariat! I vill lead them! I will be like a Gott to them! They vill be my slaves!" Any comparable signs of bad faith in *The Hairy Ape* served to distance Long from the audience and make him appear ridiculous but here, because we are allowed to perceive Hugo's self-recognition, and his attempts to hide from it, they have the reverse effect and make him seem more pitiable. His insistence on his need for sleep is a case in point. O'Neill makes this appear like some panacea clutched from childhood. Similarly, the protestation that he is drunk is repeated too often to carry convictions: "I am very trunk, no, Larry?" he says, "I talk foolishness. I am so trunk Larry, old friend, am I not, I don't know what I say? . . . Yes I should sleep. I am too crazy trunk." The very turning to another for support is expressive of his own doubt.

Because Hugo's speech is so attenuated, his words are more explicit than those of the other characters, his thoughts more immediately exposed, and so his speech acts as a kind of indicator of the general mood. This happens, for example, at the end of act 3 when Harry staggers back, having failed the challenge. Harry, as we have seen, has lost his capacity to describe his fury and fear, or to voice his subsequent despair but, because of the juxtaposition of his entrance with one of Hugo's outbursts, Hugo, who appears so oblivious of the world, is able to speak for him:

> I vill trink champagne beneath the villow—But the slaves must
> ice it properly! Gottamned Hickey! Peddler pimp for the nou-

veau riche capitalism! Vhen I lead the jackass mob to the sack
of Babylon I vill make them hang him to the nearest lamp-post
the first one! . . . I hear myself say crazy things. Do not listen,
please . . . What's matter, Harry? You look funny. You look
dead. Vhat's happened? I don't know you. Listen, I feel I am
dying, too. Because I am so crazy trunk. It is very necessary I
sleep. But I can't sleep here vith you. You look dead.

We perceive in speeches like this that O'Neill, whilst giving an impression
merely of creating speech appropriate to the speaker, is at the same time
using language to intensify the whole drama.

Hugo has one cry, "The days grow hot, O Babylon. 'Tis cool beneath
thy villow trees!" which is curiously corrupted in the speech addressed to
Harry which I have just quoted—"I vill trink champagne beneath the villow"—and which is varied by O'Neill on other occasions to give a succession of striking images in which the changing mood of the play is
epitomized. As it stands, the cry implies the remains of a revolutionary
faith of a different order from that suggested by the jargon. Whether or
not the audience recognize the source, the quotation is made available to
them in a way that the references to Nietzsche in the middle plays were
not. The phrase will be evocative for them because of its suggestion of
relief from the heat in the cool shade, and because of its echo of Psalm 137,
"By the waters of Babylon we sat down . . . we hanged our harps upon
the willows." In the convivial atmosphere of Harry's party, Hugo cries,
"Ve vill eat birthday cake and trink champagne beneath the villow trees."
When the society in Hope's bar begins to disintegrate, O'Neill demonstrates
Hugo's snobbery and the real divisions that exist between the roomers in
Hugo's substitution of "hot-dogs" and "free vine" for "cake" and "champagne" in his derisive promise of the happiness which the revolution will
bring to Rocky's group. When the general collapse is apparent, Hugo's cry,
in response to Hickey's announcement that his wife has been murdered,
"Always there is blood beneath the villow trees! I hate it and I am afraid"
is fitting, but it also expands out of the world of the play with something
of the power of poetic metaphor. At the end of the play, the audience's
relief at the return to life is qualified by their recognition that the new
optimism of the roomers is founded on Hickey's lie, and that the festivity
is a means of pushing out of mind the blood beneath the willow trees and
the dark knowledge of their own futility to which Hickey had led the
roomers. The significance which has accrued to Hugo's cry makes its emotional effect as the final line of the play terrifyingly complex. The characters

can deafen themselves by pounding their glasses and chanting together, " 'Tis cool beneath thy willow trees!," but the echo, "If I forget thee, O Jerusalem," persists in the ears of the audience.

The speech of each character, then, establishes his identity. It also contributes to the central action of the play. They interweave: figures in the same dance. And it is to their interweaving that we must now look.

The outline of the action can be given simply. In act 1, everyone waits, dreams, exists. Hickey arrives. In act 2, there is general uneasiness and the roomers veer between mutual affection and hostility. In the third act, real discord is apparent with each man concerned only for himself. The fourth act begins with each isolated from the rest, withdrawn into his own despair but, with Hickey's departure, they are able to revive their former existence. In the first act, each character's habitual mode of speech is established for the audience. Changes in that speech, in the second and third acts, convey the spiritual collapse and, at the end of the play, the revival is signalled by a return to the habitual modes. This is reductive, the dance has a liveliness we do not perceive in the notation for it, but it does demonstrate the pattern which underlies the action of *The Iceman Cometh*. The outline is filled out because of the interest O'Neill makes us feel in the lot of each of the seventeen characters. Even more important than any one individual is how credible and how valuable he makes the community appear.

The roomers in Hope's bar have their idiosyncratic speech but they also have speech in common. We saw that Larry, in the opening exchange of the play, had some American slang mixed with his Standard English. Certain slang words and phrases are shared by all the roomers. This is most noticeable amongst the words they use for alcohol and the epithets with which they address each other. Larry is the "old foolosopher," the "old wise guy" and, when Hickey christens him "old Cemetery," this name, too, is taken over by the others. Whiskey is "the booze" or "rot-gut"; they are "the bums," "the gang." They also share the language of deception. All "smoke" the same "hop," all have "pipe dreams" and, although not slang, the word "tomorrow" has special significance amongst the roomers. We saw that Larry took the word over from Rocky in the opening sequence, and thereafter it is uttered with affection by one after another character. This one will pay tomorrow, that one will go out, the other will find a job: they are all self-admitted members of the "tomorrow movement." The shared language helps us to realize not only that each man is living under a delusion, but that each deliberately reinforces the others' dreams in order to make his own dream more convincing. This collusion is the basis on which the society in Hope's bar is founded, and the shared language is, therefore, functional in communicating one of the central ideas of the play. Joe will invite everyone to the opening of his gambling house and stake them all, "If you wins, dat's velvet for you. If you loses it don't count." The sympathetic hearing of which each is confident gives him stature in his own eyes. Mosher and Mcgloin flatter Harry, who glows and willingly supports them in return. Wetjoen and Lewis dream and squabble together about their native lands. Willie suggests Mcgloin engage him as legal counsel and Mcgloin joins in the fiction, replying, "Sure I will, and it will make your reputation." The shared language shows how mutually supportive and also how artificial a construct the society is. The collapse, when it comes, seems more complete because O'Neill uses the same examples. The close friends are the first to insult each other: Joe boasts that he will return to the bar, a rich man, able to jeer at the roomers, and Mcgloin scoffs at the idea of retaining Willie's notoriously dishonest father's son as his lawyer.

Lloyd and Warfel describe people who share particular items of language as a "speech community" and make this point:

> People share speech habits in regard to matters about which they communicate with each other. Each one is thus a member of all the groups he customarily moves in, and an outsider in all the groups in which he does not. His language is a coherent system; it is all of a piece. He may not find it easy to tell which of his familiar expressions is generally known and used and which is current only in one place or among a few people.
>
> (*American English in Its Cultural Setting*)

But the audience is able to tell, because the community in Hope's bar is isolated and because O'Neill introduces an outsider who shares neither their language nor their mores. Parritt calls the roomers "tanks" which is legitimate slang for drunkards but not a word used among Hope's roomers who, we have seen, are "bums." Parritt's presence helps us to realize that the deep structure of what the roomers would say is identical although transformed at the surface in response to the idiosyncrasies of each. Addressing Parritt early in the play, Larry says, "The rules of the house are that drinks may be served at all hours." Hugo makes the same point, "Don't be a fool! Loan me a dollar! Buy me a trink!," and Willie says, "Yes, Generous Stranger—I trust you're generous." Lewis tries to catch Harry unawares by saying suddenly, "I will have a drink, now you mention it, seeing it's so near your birthday"; when Cora appears with her day's takings she immediately treats everyone to whiskey, and Hickey, finally arriving, having greeted the roomers with "Hello, gang," firmly establishes himself as one of them, whatever the subsequent action might bring, when he throws a roll of dollars on the bar and cries, "Do your duty, Brother Rocky. Bring on the rat poison." Parritt, in contrast with Hickey, is a real outsider, who hides his roll. Joe dismisses him as a "one-drink guy" and Rocky calls him "tightwad" which soon becomes the accepted name for him amongst the roomers, ostracizing him more completely. Parritt responds to the literal meaning of statements which are neutral amongst the roomers: Hugo's denunciation, "Got-tamned stool pigeon!" and Willie's confidential whisper, "No-one will ask you where you got it," are rebutted angrily by Parritt. This draws our attention to what the roomers have actually said, indicates the nature of Parritt's guilt, and also shows the emotional distance between Parritt, the isolate, and the other characters. The text leads the audience to make connections which allow the subtextual meanings to grow. When the roomers listen tolerantly to each other's pipe dreams, the clear-sighted outsider cries, "What a bunch of cuckoos!" But when, later, that outsider can find no one to listen to his self-justifying explanations of his own behaviour, we are made aware of how necessary such self-deceptions are. Parritt commits suicide partly because he exists in isolation from other men and has no social context to give him belief in himself. His is a minor role, but his presence in the play makes us more conscious of its allegorical implications.

As I have half-suggested here, Parritt is also used as a distorting mirror in which Hickey is reflected, and I will refer to this use again later, and also to his function as a catalyst who stimulates the reaction within Larry. In *Long Day's Journey into Night*, . . .the device of revealing a man's spiritual alienation by giving him the slang of a community different from the one we see on the stage is of central importance in the characterization of Jamie Tyrone.

The shared slang and the intrusive presence of Parritt convince us that the roomers form a mutually supportive community but the language is also functional in binding the audience to that community, and making it matter. Just as we enjoyed listening to Harry Hope talk, so we enjoy the atmosphere of Hope's bar. O'Neill deliberately took time to achieve this end, as a note he wrote to Macgowan reveals. He wrote, explaining why he would not cut the play:

> After all, what I've tried to write is a play where at the end you feel you know the souls of seventeen men and women who appear—and the women who don't appear— as well as if you'd

read a play about each of them. I couldn't condense much without taking a lot of life from some of these people and reducing
them to lay figures. You would find if I did not build up the
complete picture of the group as it is in the first part—the atmosphere of the place, the humour and friendship and human
warmth, the *deep inner contentment* of the bottom—you would
not be so interested in these people and you would find the
impact of what follows a lot less profoundly disturbing.

(December 13, 1940)

We have seen that in the play, O'Neill explores the dramatic potential of
American slang and of the variety of dialects found within America. In
keeping with this, we find that, in creating the atmosphere of Hope's bar,
he also draws on the traditional resources of American folk humour: jokes
based on incongruities, outrageous anecdotes and tall stories.

Stamm has claimed that *Ah, Wilderness!* is the "only one of [O'Neill's]
plays in which we find humour." It *is* the only play which might be regarded
as wholly optimistic, but that is not quite the same thing. As the audience's
reaction to any stage production bears witness, *The Iceman Cometh* is at
times extremely funny, as are all the late plays. The black depths it touches
in its presentation of human life are blacker because of the contrast with
our laughter at other moments of the play. Some of the most emotionally
harrowing moments are those which come when jokes and tall stories no
longer have power to lighten the mood.

In the first act, Joe retells Mose Porter's joke about distinguishing
anarchists from socialists, he tells the tale of Joe and de Chief, Jimmy tells
the tale of Jimmy and Dick Trumbull, Mosher tells of The Swindling of
Bessie and the tarts describe their Victories Over the Saps Outside. Each
is a dramatic narrative complete with dialogue and gesture in the tradition
of Twain's "Celebrated Jumping Frog." These tales, which become more
elaborate as they make their way towards the punch-line, demand a particular kind of attention from the audience and so help to vary the pace of
the play. One never follows immediately on another but is followed by a
quick, broken action which involves several characters: after one, a new
character enters, after another, a round of drinks is served, a friendly quarrel
breaks out. Hickey's capacity as tale-teller contributes to the enthusiasm
with which he is awaited. "What the hell you think happened to Hickey?"
says Hope, "Always got a million funny stories . . . Remember that gag
he always pulls about his wife and the Iceman? He'd make a cat laugh."

The audience warms to the characters as it laughs with them, although sometimes it is startled into awareness of its own complicity when a character draws an unexpected moral from the tale, to the delight of the others. When, for example, Mosher comments in high self-esteem after demonstrating his swindling technique, "In those days I could have short-changed the Keeper of the Mint," or when Chuck caps Cora's outrageous tale of robbing a drunken sailor with, "Ain't Uncle Sam a sap to trust guys like dat wid dough." O'Neill contrives to demonstrate the unchanging, habitual life style of the community without letting the demonstration become tedious, because of the variation. The same process operates in the shorter jokes. Early in the play Rocky makes a straight comparison, "Dis dump is like de morgue *wid all dese bums passed out.*" When Margie and Pearl enter, the comparison is turned into a quip and the common slang is replaced by a more idiosyncratic phrase, "Jees, Poil, it's de morgue *wid all de stiffs on deck,*" and, when Cora enters soon afterwards, we are treated to a picturesque elaboration, "Jees, de morgue *on a rainy Sunday night.*"

Not unexpectedly, given what we have seen of his method already, O'Neill builds on this firm basis of habitual action. Because the Iceman joke has been relished beforehand, Hickey's failure to tell it as expected disturbs the audience's as well as the roomers' expectations, and marks the beginning of his assault on the community. We recognize that Mosher is pitting the whole society against Hickey when, at the end of act 1, he temporarily restores the good humour of the community which Hickey's strange words have shattered, with a tall story about a doctor whose prescription for longevity was alcohol and no work. This draws the last burst of unstrained and unmalicious laughter until after Hickey's departure in act 4. The yarns told at the end of the play help to ensure, along with Harry's return to his robust slang, Lewis's repetition of his joke, and several similar idiosyncratic markers, that relief is one of the conflicting emotions felt by the audience at the end of the play.

But the humour also gives rise to other emotions. The audience is aware of a new harshness in the manner of the roomers towards each other in act 2. Even if they do not realize that the tales have stopped, they know that the roomers are no longer as entertaining as they were. Because of this, they probably share some of the resentment against Hickey which they see displayed on stage and are more ready to be partisan. Early in act 2, they have heard the secret suspicions Larry harbours about Hickey and, using a tension-raising device from the old melodrama, O'Neill does not scotch these suspicions at once but lets the suggestion grow in the auditors' minds. (O'Neill's relaxed attitude to melodrama and his ability to make *conscious* use of its devices is a further indication of how much more confident he is with his form than in the early years.) When Larry suddenly turns on Hickey, they are likely to be intrigued about how the question will affect Hickey's equanimity. This sequence follows:

> LARRY. I notice you didn't deny it when I asked you about the iceman. Did this great revelation of the evil habit of dreaming about tomorrow come to you after you found your wife was sick of you?
> (*While he is speaking the faces of the gang have lighted up vindictively . . .*)
> HOPE. Bejees, you've hit it, Larry! I've noticed he hasn't shown her picture around this time!
> MOSHER. He hasn't got it! The iceman took it away from him!
> MARGIE. Jees, look at him! Who could blame her?
> PEARL. She must be hard up to fall for an iceman!
> CORA. Imagine a sap like him advisin' me and Chuck to get married!
> CHUCK. Yeah! He done so good wid it!
> JIMMY. At least I can say Marjorie chose an officer and a gentleman.
> LEWIS. Come to look at you, Hickey, old chap, you've sprouted horns like a bloody antelope!
> WETJOEN. Pigger, py Gott! Like a water buffalo's!
> WILLIE. (*sings to his "Sailor Lad" tune*).
> "Come up," she cried, "my iceman lad,
> And you and I'll agree—"
> (*They all join in a jeering chorus, rapping with knuckles or glasses on the table at the indicated spot in the lyric.*)
> "And I'll show you the prettiest (*Rap, rap, rap.*)
> That ever you did see!"
> (*A roar of derisive, dirty laughter . . .*)

The audience's attention is caught by the quickened pace of the sequence, and they are likely to be propelled forward with the roomers as each brief utterance is succeeded by the next. Each familiar voice contributes its word, and one member of each of the familiar pairs, Pearl and Margie, Cora and Chuck, Wetjoen and Lewis, elaborates the remark made by the other. Together they compose a delighted and malicious substitute for the bawdy tale Hickey failed to tell on arrival. The sequence affects the audience with something of the excitement and surprise we know in the real world when several people suddenly find their minds working in concert, and the ideas accumulate to a climax in Willie's neat adaptation of his habitual song. The pattern of the sequence is broken when O'Neill directs that the whole company join in the chorus of the mocking song, supplementing the sound of their voices with loud rapping. The change gives the audience time to perceive themselves and so separates their response from that on the stage. The vision of a chanting group and a silent individual against whom they are all pitted is in itself frightening. O'Neill used it once before, in rather cruder form, to redirect the flow of empathy, when his stokers in *The Hairy Ape* were made to chant "Drink, don't think!" The three loud raps, a traditional call to attention in the theatre, also contribute to the emotional distancing of the audience, since they are likely to recall the striking suggestion made in act 1, that Willie was knocking on the door of death. I have said that shared laughter creates an emotional tie between the participants, and O'Neill here utilizes the obverse of this, which is that one-sided laughter creates a barrier. It is unlikely that the audience will laugh with the roomers at the end of Willie's song and this moment, when enjoyment is not shared, establishes a doubt about the nature of the society in Hope's bar which will coexist for the rest of the play with the positive response to that society which we have already noted. When Hickey replies to the mockery with the announcement that his wife is dead, the roomers are silenced and shamed and the audience are made more acutely aware of their own brief complicity in the persecution, and are, therefore, alerted to future ambiguities in the action.

A problem with this kind of commentary is that, because the play is broken into constituent parts, it appears more schematic than it is in performance when everything is closely interlocked and the audience receives a continuous flow of suggestions, echoes and images. The first distorted version of the iceman joke, for example, created here by the whole community is echoed by a second. Hickey's confession in the fourth act is, in effect, a longer, more chilling and more serious version of it. Part of the reason why we listen with such fascination to the confession, and it lasts for a quarter of an hour of performance time—an extraordinarily long time—is that we have been so well prepared, for the method, by the tales of the first act and, for its emotional impact, by this sequence at the end of act 2. We will have already been alerted to the possibility that there is allegorical meaning in the references to "the iceman" because the word appears in the title of the play and so we will take the association of the iceman with death from the juxtaposition of the roomers' taunting joke with Hickey's announcement. Alerted by sequences such as the one under discussion, the frequent references to death in the play begin to press in upon us. At first, we have been scarcely more conscious of the death imagery in the jokes and slang of the roomers than we are of the latent metaphor in everyday words. "Kill a pint"; "It's a dead cinch"; "When I don't want a drink, you call the morgue"; "What is this, a funeral?"—we don't count off such expressions as they occur, nor do we anxiously seek out their meanings, but, by their very frequency, they serve to provide a context within which the more directly relevant statements: "Would that Hickey or Death would come"; "Death was the Iceman Hickey called to his home," reverberate. As the community in Hope's bar crumbles, we find ourselves convinced by the cold touch Hickey has introduced there and we recognize it as the touch not of physical but of spiritual death.

A comparison between the first and final drafts of this sequence demonstrates how the play took on significance in the writing. The scene was mapped out in the scenario in this way.

> Larry (suddenly). How's your wife, Hickey?—Hickey (startled). What makes you ask about her? Larry (with amused carelessness). You always used to talk about her, show photo—H. Never when I was sober. But thank you for enquiring. Evelyn is taking a long, much deserved rest.—Margie, A vacation, you mean,—with the iceman?—H. (with a strange smile). Yes, I think you might say she is in the arms of the iceman. I'm sorry to have to tell you that my dear wife is dead. At once, all except Larry full of contrition.

As originally conceived, only one character besides Larry contributed. There is no suggestion in the scenario of a change in tempo, nor of the malice of the final text. There is nothing to implicate the audience. Hickey's metaphorical play on the word "iceman" at this juncture allows a much less subtle subsequent development than the juxtaposition later adopted by O'Neill. Similarly, it was originally intended that the tension at the end of act 1 should be relaxed not by Mosher's somewhat inconsequential tall story, but by all the roomers joining in with Hugo's cry. Had this been retained, the final chant of the play would have been a direct echo of it and would therefore have recalled a moment of relief. This would have given the play something of the mechanical regularity of the early plays. In writing, the pattern lost such easy symmetry. By transferring the first use of voices in chorus to act 2 and using the device in the menacing way it is used, O'Neill makes the final chant echo an emotionally ambivalent rather than an optimistic moment of the play. The ending of the play is correspondingly more complex as a result.

Before I leave *The Iceman Cometh* I want to comment on the role of language in the characterization of Larry Slade who, as I have suggested, is a more rounded character than the others and, as such, gives a foretaste of the characterization in *Long Day's Journey into Night*. I may seem, in leaving the discussion of the other characters where I have, to have given some of them, particularly Hickey, short shrift, but I think that once the method is clear, it is readily applicable to each of the characterizations. Although Hickey's role is much the largest in the play, his language parallels that of the other figures. His presence causes their disintegration but, at a later stage of the play, he disintegrates in just the way they have done. What strikes us most forcibly about his speech, and this is consistent throughout the play, is the contrast between its restlessness and the peace he preaches. The language of efficient salesmanship sits as ill with his message as it does when associated with the Christian message in some brands of evangelical religion, as O'Neill himself reminds us in Hickey's references to his preacher father (see act 4). The essential point made by his language is that he is one with the roomers.

At one level Larry, too, is one with the roomers and elements in the shared language of the bar which apply directly to him, help to make his presence there credible. I described the principal idiosyncrasies of Larry's speech in my discussion of the opening scene of the play, and will just add to that a note about his Irishness since, although not noticeable there, we do become aware of it in other parts of the play and its use foreshadows that in *Long Day's Journey into Night*. The Irish dialect marker "sure," used to begin a sentence, is occasionally added to Larry's Standard English. It is used entirely to signal light banter, and we are left in no doubt that it is deliberately assumed by Larry since, when he flatters Pearl and Margie with "Sure, I love every hair of your heads, my great big beautiful baby dolls," Pearl comments, "De old Irish bunk, huh?" But without making an obvious point of Larry's Irishness, O'Neill flavours his speech and suggests the fluency of Irish English. This effect seems to derive from the choice of one kind of word order rather than another. He forms questions, for example, by means of subject/predicator inversion: "Isn't a pipe dream of yesterday a touching thing?" "Didn't I tell you he'd brought death with him?" rather than by the addition of a clause: "I told you he'd brought death with him, didn't I?" Either form is equally acceptable in Standard English, but the former is used far more frequently by Larry. In this sentence pattern, the stressed question word leads us into the sentence and allows the significant word to come in the rising cadence at the end of the sentence. It lends itself more readily to being spoken with an "Irish lilt." A similar pattern of stress and cadence derives from Larry's frequent use of introductory phrases, "Be God," "By all accounts," "What the hell."

Larry stands in a different relation to the audience from the other figures, because in the early part of the play he acts as a narrator. He is positioned at the side of the stage, from where he describes the bar and its inhabitants to the outsider, Parritt. In the original plan for the play, Larry was not affected by Hickey's mission but was to be an observer of it. In some notes dated June 1939, we find him described in this way: "Terry— who sees and is articulate about real meaning of what is going on—who regrets they can't leave themselves alone—can't forgive themselves for not being what they are not." As we have seen, the play, born out of O'Neill's nostalgia, was much slighter and more benign in its original conception than in its final form. No internal conflict is stirred in Larry in the scenario by the presence of Potter [Parritt] and he bears no responsibility for the younger man's suicide, which comes as a direct response, not to him but to the typical cry from Hap [Hugo], "Traitor to the gallows!" Larry merely comments, "Justice has taken its course," before joining the other roomers in their festivity, with the words, "out of great drunkenness, comes great wisdom." The character grew in the writing, although the role of narrator, retained from the original conception, helps to distance Larry and prevents our concern with his private struggle from becoming the central issue.

The Larry of the play differs from the other roomers in that we seem to see more fully into his consciousness. This impression derives in part from the tenor of his speech. So many of his utterances are warnings to the others, to distinguish poison from "the real McCoy," to drink themselves oblivious of Hickey, that he seems to take responsibility for their fate. He wrestles with Hickey on their behalf, "Leave Hugo be . . . Have you no decency or pity?" and they in their turn admit their distress to him, "It's been hell in that damned room, Larry," "I'm glad you're here, Larry." The result is that, when we see their individual torment, we are also aware of Larry, sitting at the side of the stage, sharing their suffering. But the image of Larry is complicated by the presence of Parritt. Parritt is increasingly identified with Larry, since he addresses his words almost entirely to the old anarchist. He addresses Larry familiarly from the outset, although Larry never uses his name in return, and the disparity alerts us to Larry's attempt to hide. Parritt is a reflection of some aspects of Hickey and frequently is used to relay Hickey's words to Larry with a taunting, "What did he mean by that, Larry?," "What do you say to that, Larry?" His presence on the stage serves to project Larry's internal conflict. Under pressure from Parritt, Larry becomes terse and avoids direct replies. When he becomes almost completely silent in act 4, Parritt's voice, mocking, challenging, pleading, keeps Larry's struggle in the audience's mind and, at the tensest moment of Hickey's confession, there, too, is Parritt, whispering his confession, for Larry's ear alone.

The state of Larry's consciousness is revealed also through the very structure of his speech. His style becomes plainer when he is disturbed, and his syntax is organized to convey the unconscious processes of his thought. In the example here, I have separated the sentences and italicized certain words in order to demonstrate this point more clearly:

> It's nothing to me what happened to him.
> But I have a feeling he's dying to tell us, inside him, and yet
> he's *afraid*.
> He's like that damned kid.
> It's strange the queer way he seems to recognize him.
> If he's *afraid*, it explains why he's off booze.
> Like that damned kid again.
> *Afraid* if he got drunk, he'd tell—

As the recurrent adjective moves to the beginning of the sentence, the idea of fear is expressed first as an afterthought, then as a supposition and, finally, as a positive statement. This implies a preoccupation with Hickey on Larry's part which contradicts his first statement, "It's nothing to me." The repetition of the reference to the "kid" shows in a similar way how dark a shadow Parritt's presence has cast upon his mind. Larry scarcely participates in the opening exchange of act 4, although he has figured prominently in parallel sequences of earlier acts. What he does say confirms the impression his silence gives, of his extreme anxiety. His replies to the demands of other characters are all denials, "No, it doesn't look good," "I don't think anything," "Stop shoving your rotten soul in my lap." After a hopeless attempt to prevent Hickey's confession, he does not speak again until after Hickey has gone. The contrast with his former readiness to comment on any eventuality draws our attention to him and, when his suffering finally spills over into words, we feel it the more fiercely because the words Parritt has begged from him are scarcely coherent, "Go! Get the hell out of life! God damn you, before I choke it out of you! Go up—!" The two oaths in quick succession show how remote his present speech is from his earlier care and delight in elaboration, and the alliteration here does not decorate but serves to increase the choked staccato effect of the exclamations. The self-contradictory nature of Larry's last speech reveals his final position more fully than does the meaning of the individual words. His speech has become what Blackmur has called "the language of gesture."

The verbal gesturing, indeed, interacts with and draws meaning from the physical gesture and the stage picture. The tables and chairs in Hope's bar have been slightly redistributed between acts 1 and 4, as O'Neill's own sketches for the stage plan make clear. The redistribution marks the difference between the easy, aimless atmosphere in the bar at the opening of the play, and the roomers' clustering together for support at the end. First Hickey leaves his position at the middle of the stage, then Parritt exists from the table at Left Front, so that there is an imbalance in the distribution of characters on the stage. The imbalance is emphasized when Hugo, in the last minutes of the play, moves across to join the other roomers and, in doing so, leaves Larry isolated in his corner of the stage.

The fact that Larry is revealed so fully does not contradict the logic of the play since his illusion is ontological and, of necessity, when Hickey strikes at it, he strikes at Larry's very mode of thought. But it does place Larry in a special relationship to the audience and makes his role a vital one in their perception of the action. When he continues to sit absolutely still and apart during the sequence in which the roomers reconstitute their lives he, the only one to have accepted the consequences of Hickey's message, seems to absorb into himself all their former despair. He becomes the spectre at the feast, the image of everyone's reality.

The Iceman Cometh and Modern Society

John Orr

While [O'Neill] had been willing to cut earlier plays like *Strange Interlude* for commercial purposes, he was adamant that in its first production *The Iceman* should run its full length of nearly four and a half hours. For most directors, the temptation to cut it must be very great. The play is deliberately repetitive and rhetorical and at times restatement seems to add little to what has already been expressed. But the strength of the play is cumulative like a musical symphony. The restatement and recurrence are progressive. Taken together action and dialogue have an almost operatic impact upon the eye and the ear. Out of this cumulative strength the immense power of the play's tragic climax unfolds. It is *The Iceman,* not *Mourning Becomes Electra,* which approximates most closely to the lyrical and auratic power of Greek tragedy.

One thing which stands out, and makes the play a masterpiece of its own age, is the extraordinary use of the choric device. The inhabitants of Harry Hope's backroom bar are not merely a choral appendage to Hickey, the salesman, but have their own collective destiny. They are both collective hero and dissonant chorus to their own fate. The final euphoric chant of the play is shouted in "enthusiastic jeering chorus":

> The days grow hot, O Babylon!
> 'Tis cool beneath the willow trees!

Out of dissonance and chaos, it reaffirms the collective identity and the collective experience of the ensemble. The musical harmonies here and

From *Tragic Drama and Modern Society.* © 1981 by John Orr. Macmillan, 1981.

throughout recall Chekhov, and by contrast the one play with which *The Iceman* has been systematically compared, Gorky's *The Lower Depths,* seems chaotically ill-composed.

There is no doubt that the Russian play had been a formative influence on O'Neill's writing. He saw it as the outstanding example of revolutionary proletarian drama in the twentieth century, and the borrowing of the play's theme is obvious. But merely to see the difference between the two plays in terms of their ending, contrasting Gorky's optimism and O'Neill's pessimism, is rather myopic. The more central difference lies in the role of the major protagonist in each play. Whereas Luka mysteriously disappears after having set into motion the actions and suspicions leading to the breakdown of community, Hickey himself is the tragic figure of O'Neill's drama remaining at the centre of the dramatic action until his fate is sealed. Both are redeemers but the crucial shift of role is clearly apparent. While Luka is a mere catalyst, Hickey is a tragic protagonist. Because the link between the redeemer and the collective is more organic, it is also more tragic. In this respect, Hickey is closer in sensibility and enactment to Gregers Werle. Though it appears deceptively simple at times, the salesman's idealism is equally complex, and its appropriate dramatic expression is integral to the success of the play.

This complexity is sometimes obscured by the performance of Hickey as a frantic evangelical salesman obsessed by his own powers of exhortation. His extended speeches are then delivered one-dimensionally in an exhortatory manner with little variation in rhythm or tone. But vary they must, as sharply in places as the mood of Ella Downey or Mary Tyrone. This complexity can be just as easily obscured by critical references to the religious model upon which the confrontation of Hickey and the drunken roomers is based—that of Christ and his disciples at the Last Supper. For Hickey is more than a failed Christ figure come to visit his twelve reluctant disciples, and offer them salvation. The whole play should be seen more as a Nietzschean negation of the New Testament myth in which the redeemer himself is insane and actively attempts to deny the redemption he offers. On a metaphysical level, the denial of redemption leads to the hero's madness. Hickey is both Christ and Antichrist, saving no one, yet finally himself crucified.

The dramatic context of the denial of redemption, is not, however, metaphysical. It is social. In the relationship between the expectant barflies and the magnanimous salesman, O'Neill establishes a social correlative fundamental to the United States of his own lifetime. It is the relationship between the purgatory of social failure and the promise of the American

Dream. The sense of squalor and degradation is perhaps not as great as in Gorky. But the sense of social downfall is correspondingly stronger, and the feel of that downward movement is preserved in Larry Slade's pronouncement to Parritt, the young newcomer to the bar:

> What is it? It's the No Chance Saloon. It's Bedrock Bar, the End of the Line Café, the Bottom of the Sea Rathskeller. Don't you notice the beautiful calm in the atmosphere? That's because it's the last harbour. No one here has to worry about where they're going next because there is no farther they can go

Yet there is an important addendum to this grim image of finality. Even at the lowest level of spiritual and material existence, it remains impossible to live without some residual hope: "Even here they keep up the appearance of life with a few harmless pipe dreams about their yesterdays and tomorrows." The keyword is "pipe dream." It occurs a myriad of times during the course of the play from the mouth of almost every figure even when, as is usually the case, its existence is being vehemently denied.

At the beginning of the play the arrival of Hickey is awaited with great eagerness, not only because he has the money to buy round after round of drinks, but because he has the knack of encouraging a drunken camaraderie that the inmates of the saloon are too demoralised to generate of their own accord. The reform of his character, announced soon after his arrival, comes as a complete shock to them and suggests an imminent confrontation. The hard-drinking narrator of dirty jokes appears to have turned into a moral crusader exhorting them to give up their alcoholic ways and make the effort to return to their former more productive lives. To this extent Hickey does resemble Luka in Gorky's play. But the resemblance is only superficial. Beneath Hickey's evangelism is a hidden dimension which makes it apparent that the crusade is part of a strategy, at best a ruse to help reveal to the inmates a more fundamental aspect of their existence. For Hickey expects each of them in turn to fail to come to terms with the outside world, and to return one by one to the backroom bar, dejected and defeated. It then becomes clear that Hickey is not the reformed salesman of the American Dream but something more sinister. The prophet of the ideology of individual self-help and success emerges as the very opposite, a harbinger of destruction who by his action unmasks the very ideology to which he appears to bear allegiance.

His idealism is not, like that of Gregers, based purely on a fundamental misreading of the lives of others, but on the false connection he makes between his own experience and what he is demanding of them. He wants them to kill off their pipe dreams of a better tomorrow because he himself has already been forced to do so:

> I've been through the mill and had to face a worse bastard in myself than any of you will have to in yourselves. I know you become such a coward you'll grab at any excuse to get out of killing your pipe dreams. And yet, as I've told you over and over, it's exactly those same damned tomorrow dreams which keep you from making peace with yourself. So you've got to kill them like I did mine.

Like Gregers, Hickey is attempting the impossible. But whereas Gregers can blithely ignore the accusation of his failure at the end of the play, Hickey's very life depends on the possibility of success in his enterprise. His attempt to reveal to the roomers their fundamental inadequacy is the prelude to an even more extraordinary revelation of his own failure. His self–confession is not an intentional unmasking, but an unintended result of his failure to unmask and exorcise the pipe dreams of others. Once doubt begins to creep into the whole enterprise, the mask begins to slip from his face. Slade, the ex-anarchist philosopher, the most intellectual of the roomers and the one with the most to lose, first recognises the weakness. The process of counterexposure then begins. After Harry Hope, venturing outside the saloon for the first time in twenty years, stops dead in the middle of the street and scurries back like a frightened rabbit, the peace which Hickey promised him by exorcising his pipe dream seems as far away as ever:

> HOPE (*dully*). What's wrong with this booze? There's no kick in it.
> ROCKY (*worriedly*). Jees, Larry, Hugo had it right. He does look like he'd croaked.
> HICKEY (*annoyed*). Don't be a damned fool! Give him time. He's coming along all right. (*He calls to Hope with a first trace of underlying uneasiness.*) You're all right aren't you, Harry?
> HOPE (*dully*). I want to pass out like Hugo.
> LARRY (*turns to Hickey with bitter anger*). It's the peace of death you've brought him!
> HICKEY (*for the first time loses his temper*). That's a lie! (*But he controls this instantly and grins.*) Well, well you did manage to get a rise out of me that time.

Slade has at last come to understand the extreme nihilism of Hickey's vision. The alternative to the alcoholic pipe dream, the residue of the ideal as O'Neill conceives it, is death. The illusory peace of which Hickey has spoken is permanent oblivion. Hickey's vision also has repercussions for the dramatic action itself. What it entails is a total destruction of the last elements of figural prophecy. The pipe dreams of the roomers are the essential base condition for that figural sense to be conveyed as dramatic action. The dramatic space of the play depends on them and is paradoxically enlarged by Hickey's attempt to destroy them, for the drunken choric elements of the action, whether as rambling reminiscence or absurd aspiration are both thematically and aesthetically indestructible. Inevitably, Hickey must fail. There is then a dual basis for the creation of Hickey as a tragic figure. Not only is his dream a dream to end all human dreams, his destructiveness, if successful, would annihilate tragedy itself. The general failure to destroy tragedy turns him into a tragic hero. O'Neill has explored in his play the bedrock conditions for the figural dramatisation of human life and the *figura* is vindicated.

Thematically speaking, the tragic nature of Hickey's failure arises from his own involvement in the life he preaches for others. He tries to mould the inmates after the pattern of his own concealed destiny, and when that fails, has to reveal on the point of madness his own failure—the murder of his wife. Unlike Melville's confidence man who is the sum of all his ingenious disguises with no basic self, it is Hickey's intractable self which is his own undoing. The confession to murder turns the inspired crusader into a helpless crazed victim, waiting to be led away by detectives to trial and to the electric chair while the inmates of the "No Chance Saloon" are made aware in amazement of a worse fate than their own which they have managed to avoid. In a wider context, Hickey's crusade *against* the American Dream is similar to Nietzsche's incestuous revolt against Christian redemption. It mirrors the pattern of the redemptive crusade by turning bitterly and uncompromisingly against it. Yet it retains the style and the pattern while forsaking the substance, and disintegrates into insanity.

The relevance of the subplot to the main action is not always apparent because of its dramatic looseness, but in the last act it helps to throw into focus both the power of Hickey's vision and its relation to revolutionary idealism. The subplot hinges upon a particular kind of absence crucial to the play—that of women except as prostitutes. Both Hickey's murdered wife and Parritt's betrayed mother have a white purity of absent virtue, a virtue in fact which sometimes strains credibility, but at the same time exempts their sex from the self-betrayals which brought their menfolk to the "No Chance Saloon." Parritt's guilt at betraying his mother and the Movement to the authorities, and Slade's subsequent refusal to recognise Parritt as his son, are often clumsy diversions from the main dramatic development. But ultimately they dovetail with the main plot since Larry combines a growing recognition of Hickey's dementia with a stubborn refusal to face the truth about Parritt, and in so doing reveals the link between the insight of intellect and the weakness of personality.

Slade's growing awareness of Hickey's role as a messenger of death is connected with the years of political activism he has spent and now rejected in disillusionment. Because of this political connection, he is the most ideologically resistant to Hickey and yet in the end, the only one who is really seduced. His vulnerability can only be understood in the context of his earlier rejection of the movement, a rejection he makes explicit to Parritt at great length:

> One was myself, and another was my comrades and the last was the breed of swine called men in general. For myself I was forced to admit, at the end of thirty years' devotion to the Cause, that I was never made for it. I was born condemned to be one of those who had to see all sides of a question. When you're damned like that, the questions multiply for you until in the end it's all question and no answer! As history proves, to be a worldly success at anything, especially revolution, you have to wear blinkers like a horse and see only straight in front of you. You have to see, too, that this is all black, and that is all white. As for my comrades in the Great Cause, I felt as Horace Walpole did about England that he could love it if it weren't for the people in it. The material the ideal free society must be constructed from is men themselves and you can't build a marble temple out of a mixture of mud and manure. When a man's soul isn't a sow's ear, it will be time enough to dream of silk purses.

His ability to see through the pretensions of the Movement gives him the resources to resist Hickey's crusade, but his disenchantment with the Movement and the apathy that disenchantment engenders make him vulnerable to Hickey's message of lasting peace with oneself. The peace Hickey offers eliminates the political contradiction which has always haunted Slade. As he remarks at the end, death is the only real alternative to his basic weakness, "the fool looking with pity at two sides of everything till the day I die!" He is, in his own words, "the only real convert to death Hickey ever made."

Why does Slade lack the power of the other roomers to survive? The answer is that his past failures are more haunting and absolute. While the play cannot be seen as a parable about the failure of American socialism—especially since Slade, Hugo and Parritt represent a more anarchistic faction—it does transmit a deep sense of opportunity lost and never again to be offered. The life remembered joins the political failure to the social and the personal and it was the nearest that O'Neill ever came to writing full-length political drama. But the tragic alienation he engenders derives precisely from an absolute withdrawal. Harry Hope's saloon is a refuge for the apolitical and the antisocial, and there can be no possibility of reabsorption. Even Hickey, though he pretends not to, realises this. The saloon represents a residual but invincible affront to the ideals of American life, not by casting them into oblivion but by clinging to them with a stubborn perversity and at the same time, distorting them out of all recognition. The transformation from alienation to strife occurs with Hickey's failure to annihilate the grotesquerie of the ideal, the barroom pipe dream, and the horrified recognition of what that quest for annihilation means in normal social life. What Hickey demands of the inmates is exemplified in a normal respectable social context by the murder of his devoted and forgiving wife. The tragic horror conveyed to them as outcast chorus is the transgression of the normal by their would-be redeemer, and this transgression is greater than anything they themselves have managed to accomplish.

O'Neill's work here goes beyond questions of political idealism and disenchantment. It expresses a profound concern with the impact of capitalism on the American way of life, an impact which has persisted throughout the century despite, and sometimes because of, the vagaries of political opposition. While revolutionary idealism has been volatile and at times perfidious, the system to which it is a response has prevailed permanently in all areas of life. In O'Neill's mature work this was the guarantor of tragic alienation and its transformation to a fully realised tragic strife. But the work was historical within the span of O'Neill's lifetime since the constancy of his opposition to the American way of life was tempered by the sense of lost promise. The latter gives the vital historical dimension to the former which is both historical and contemporary, a part of time past and time present and also of our own age, time future, when the themes of the play strike a chord of instant recognition through their profoundly prophetic qualities.

Endings

Normand Berlin

Between 1916 (*Bound East for Cardiff*) and 1934 (*Days without End*) O'Neill had a full and varied theatrical life. Within these years Broadway saw thirty-four of his plays; on thirty-three of these (*Dynamo* excepted) O'Neill worked closely until their production, attending rehearsals, making last-minute changes, talking with directors and actors. That is, he was actively involved not only in the writing but also in the production of his plays. Had he stopped writing in 1934, his reputation as America's finest dramatist would have remained positive. *Days without End* could have ended the career of a dramatist who had totally committed himself to his art, who was exhausted, physically and perhaps spiritually (despite the "positive" ending of *Days without End*), and who could have rested on the laurels of the past, justifiably proud of his considerable accomplishment. What is remarkable is that O'Neill—silent for twelve years, with no new O'Neill play to appear on Broadway until 1946—is now ready to write the plays of his history cycle, a task left unfinished, *and* to write the four plays that are among his finest accomplishments—*The Iceman Cometh, Hughie, Long Day's Journey into Night, A Moon for the Misbegotten*. These last four plays, the endings of his tortuous journey, crown O'Neill's formidable career. They mark a change in his artistic development and they form a unit, although they also carry on many of his former theatrical techniques and expand on many of his characteristic themes. The most striking analogue to O'Neill's accomplishment in this last phase is Shakespeare's accomplishment in his last romances, also the stunning climax of a formidable career, also a change in mode,

From *Eugene O'Neill*. © 1982 by Normand Berlin. Macmillan, 1982.

also comprising a unit, and also a continuation of much that went before. Merely citing the analogue points to the extent of O'Neill's remarkable achievement.

The span of five years (1939 through 1943) in which he wrote the last four plays were difficult years for O'Neill (because of personal illness) and difficult years for the world. Hitler was on the march; Germany invaded Poland in 1939, when *The Iceman Cometh* was being written. (In a sense, Hitler was the world's "iceman.") Britain and France declared war on Germany. America entered the conflict in 1941, the year in which O'Neill completed *Long Day's Journey*. O'Neill's mood at this time can only be described as despairing. Surely, the miserable state of the world was an important reason for his twelve-year silence from the stage. During this period O'Neill looked more deeply within, and confronted more directly man's existential nature. During this period O'Neill wrote his most "modern" plays, presenting a vision of man not too far from that of Samuel Beckett. It is not surprising, therefore, that the complex plays of his last period have received the most critical attention, and that they were the basis for his revival in 1956. *The Iceman Cometh,* which in 1946 ended O'Neill's absence from Broadway, is the very play which begins O'Neill's revival ten years later. *The Iceman Cometh,* therefore, occupies a very important place in O'Neill's career, but its value as a work of dramatic art goes far beyond any considerations based on development or reputation. *The Iceman Cometh* joins *Long Day's Journey* as a masterpiece. It allows the name O'Neill to be mentioned along with Ibsen, Strindberg, Chekhov, Shaw, and perhaps one or two others, as the giants of modern drama.

The year of the play is 1912, the year of *Long Day's Journey,* and the setting, like that of *Long Day's Journey,* encloses its characters in a world that seems isolated. In *The Iceman Cometh,* however, we are not in the living-room of a New England summer house, but in a "dying" saloon in New York City, accurately described by Larry Slade early in the play:

> It's the No Chance Saloon. It's Bedrock Bar, The End of the Line Cafe, the Bottom of the Sea Rathskeller! Don't you notice the beautiful calm in the atmosphere? That's because it's the last harbor. No one here has to worry about where they're going next, because there is no farther they can go.

(Immediately, O'Neill is pointing the realistic toward the symbolic, as he did in his early plays, with the Sea a source for metaphor.) In *The Iceman Cometh* we meet not a family of four Tyrones, but another kind of family, more than a dozen lodgers in Harry Hope's saloon who share two characteristics—they are all kept alive by alcohol and by "pipe dreams,"—with the latter perhaps more important than the former. According to the play's main witness and spokesman, Larry Slade—the only lodger who is not asleep, the Irishman with a strain of bitter humor, whose face expresses the "tired tolerance" of "a pitying but weary old priest"—"the lie of the pipe dream is what gives life to the whole misbegotten mad lot of us, drunk or sober." That is why the seedy derelicts are in *Hope*'s saloon, symbolism and realism always mingling. The minds of all the roomers are soaked in alcohol, but their illusions—the phrase "pipe dream" is repeated relentlessly—sustain them.

Each derelict has a separate dream: Harry Hope wishes to return to ward politics, Ed Mosher to the circus, Hugo Kalmar to leadership in the "revolution"—his "The days grow hot, O Babylon! / 'Tis cool beneath thy willow trees!" becoming a kind of refrain for both revolution and death—Joe Mott (the last of O'Neill's blacks) to proprietorship of a gambling house, Jimmy Tomorrow—who was modeled on James Byth, O'Neill's friend who committed suicide Parritt-style by jumping from a fire escape at Jimmy the Priest's saloon—to a respectable job in journalism, and so on. Each of the roomers has a past which produced the dreadful present. The self-respect of each *depends upon* the belief that tomorrow will change today, that the pipe dream will come true. When they are forced by Hickey to face the "truth" of their lives, they become hostile and isolated and despairing. Only when they return at play's end to the pipe dream do they become a family again. They end as they began—O'Neill ever fond of the circle—frozen to their conditions and their seats, whiskey-soaked, talking of tomorrow. The play's thesis: the truth destroys, man needs illusion in order to live, self-knowledge (that Apollonian ideal) can kill. Unquestionably, *The Iceman Cometh* is a thesis play, offering as blatant a message as O'Neill's didactic plays of the late twenties, but here O'Neill allows emotion to fuel his ideas and even to transcend his ideas. Here his technique—combining realism and symbolism (the old combination of his "beginnings" and of the forceful plays of the early twenties, but refined and deepened) and offering much comedy—allows O'Neill to break out of a mechanical thesis mold. In this story of crime and punishment, O'Neill presents a powerful drama of surprising variety, considering the absence of exciting action, the bareness of the plot, the reliance on just talk, the somnolent, inert state of almost all the characters, and the simplicity of the thesis. O'Neill exploits those old "theatrical" standbys—expectation, conflict between two strong personalities (Hickey and Larry), variety of character—and a "classical" standby, the unity of time, place, and action. The play manages to *say* something because the truth of O'Neill's statement emerges genuinely and gracefully from the emotional life of his drama.

The play's title could have been "Waiting for Hickey" because Hickey's arrival is eagerly expected through most of act 1, and because Hickey causes whatever happens in the play to happen. That he will be coming to Harry Hope's birthday celebration is the common topic of comment and discussion for all the derelicts. Hickey, when he comes twice a year, is always good for a few drinks and for many laughs. He is a salesman with a gift of gab, someone who knows how to size up people and how to liven up a party with his crude salesman jokes. His crudest and favorite joke, according to the bar bums, is that he left his wife Evelyn in bed with the iceman. They look forward to seeing him and to hearing that joke again. When he arrives toward the end of act 1, he will be more sober and serious than the Hickey they knew, and the iceman joke will have ominous implications. But O'Neill delays his coming for a long time, building up an interest in the unseen character, and offers hints here and there of the import of his arrival, the most explicit of which is the comment of Willie Oban, the youngest of the derelicts, the intellectual Harvard Law School graduate: "Let us join in prayer that Hickey, the Great Salesman, will soon arrive bringing the blessed bourgeois long green! Would that Hickey or Death would come!" By forcing the derelicts to face themselves, Hickey will bring "death" instead of salvation; he will put them on ice, so to speak. And when we learn in act 4 that he killed his wife Evelyn, he becomes the Iceman who sleeps with his wife, the Iceman of the play's title, Death. Dudley Nichols, a writer and a friend of O'Neill, says this about the title:

> The iceman of the title is, of course, death. I don't think O'Neill ever explained, publicly, what he meant by the use of the archaic word, "cometh," but he told me at the time he was writing the play that he meant a combination of the poetic and biblical "Death cometh"—that is, cometh to all living things—and the old bawdy story, a typical Hickey story, of the man who calls upstairs, "Has the iceman come yet?" and his wife calls back, "No, but he's breathin' hard." Even the bawdy story is transformed by the poetic intention of the title, for it is really Death which Hickey's wife, Evelyn, has taken to her breast when she marries Hickey, and her insistence on her great love for Hickey and his undying love for her and her deathlike grip on his conscience—her insistence that he *can* change and not get drunk and sleep with whores—is making Death breathe hard on her breast as he approaches ever nearer—as he is about "to come" in the

vernacular sense. It is a strange and poetic intermingling of the exalted and the vulgar, that title.

This mixture of the crude and the biblical mirrors the realistic-symbolic nature of the play. Hickey's arrival is so long in coming, takes on such significance when it comes, that he should be considered a particular hardware salesman and *more than* a salesman, or, to use Willie Oban's phrase, the "Great Salesman." Waiting for Hickey is like waiting for Godot, and in both O'Neill and Beckett the waiters are in a frozen condition, a boundary situation. At play's end, Beckett leaves his Didi and Gogo waiting for Godot; in O'Neill, however, Godot *comes*—with the kind of bursting explosion we associate with the word "come" when we think in sexual terms, with the explosion of death when we think of Hickey killing his wife, with the destruction of illusions when we think of his preachments to the down-and-outers. He has reformed, and this son of a preacher will now attempt to reform his friends at Harry Hope's; he will bring them the kind of "peace" he has found because he has had "the guts to face myself."

When the lodgers are forced by Hickey's insistence to face themselves, when he destroys their pipe dreams, they figuratively die. Even the whiskey no longer has a kick. By selling the truth, Hickey the Salesman was selling death without realizing it. His own pipe dream, that he loved his wife Evelyn, momentarily becomes shattered when he—during a long confessional speech taking fifteen minutes of stage time—reveals that he laughed when he killed Evelyn and said to her: "Well, you know what you can do with your pipe dream now, you damned bitch!" This is the moment of discovery for Hickey. His pipe dream, that he loved his wife, is a lie; he hated her for the guilt she made him feel. He killed her to rid himself of her forgiveness and his guilt. But this momentary revelation, this unconscious slip which forces him to face his true motive in killing his wife, does not lead Hickey to accept the truth about himself. His was the biggest pipe dream of all—that he loved his wife. Now he cannot face the truth of his hatred, so he says, "Good God, I couldn't have said that! If I did, I'd gone insane! Why, I loved Evelyn better than anything in life!" He leaves the stage—accompanied by police officers whom he called and who heard his confession—pleading insanity, not to escape punishment, as they seem to think, but because his pipe dream persists. Just as the derelicts return to their pipe dreams—latching on to Hickey's insanity as the reason for his strange behavior and his lies about them—so Hickey returns to his. For the derelicts, the whiskey has a bite again, and they can sink into the illusions about yesterday and tomorrow that they possessed in the play's beginning.

But two characters cannot be so easily comforted. Don Parritt, the

eighteen-year-old outsider, has come to Harry Hope's saloon to see Larry
Slade, who intimately knew Parritt's mother, Rose, a leading member of
an anarchist movement. His mother was betrayed to the police, and this
freedom-loving woman will be spending the rest of her life in prison. As
the play progresses, Parritt admits to Larry that he betrayed the movement,
but did not realize his mother would be caught. Later, he says he knew
she'd be caught but he needed the money he received for betraying her.
Then—while Hickey is confessing his murder—Parritt parrots Hickey by
blurting out that he betrayed his mother because he hated her. But, whereas
Hickey pleads insanity, Parritt receives the words he wants to hear from
Larry—"Go! Get the hell out of life, God damn you, before I choke it out
of you! Go up—!"—and commits suicide by jumping from the upstairs fire
escape. Parritt's guilt leads him to punish himself; he has no pipe dream to
keep him alive.

Larry too no longer has a pipe dream at play's end, thanks to Parritt's
suicide, which makes Larry realize he is *involved* with others, and thanks
to Hickey's taunting throughout the play. Larry and Hickey are the play's
protagonists. In a play of many minor conflicts between different personalities—with so huge a cast such conflicts are inevitable—Larry and Hickey
provide the play's major conflict: Hickey is selling the truth; Larry is up-
holding the necessity of the pipe dream. Larry exclaims: "To hell with the
truth! As the history of the world proves, the truth has no bearing on
anything. It's irrelevant and immaterial, as the lawyers say." He believes
"The tomorrow movement is a sad and beautiful thing too!" He does
nothing to dampen the illusions of his fellow bums in "The End of the
Line Cafe"; he allows them to wallow in their boozy dreams. Larry realizes
the consequences of Hickey's proselytizing assault on the lodgers, and tries
to prevent him from hurting them. He is filled with pity for his fellow
creatures, which puts him in direct conflict with Hickey, who believes that
Larry's kind of pity is injurious. But Larry has his weakness too, for he
believes he has no illusions (they are "dead and buried behind me"), that
he wants to die ("death is a fine long sleep, and I'm damned tired, and it
can't come too soon for me"), and that he is merely an observer of mankind,
never getting involved, taking a seat "in the grandstand of philosophical
detachment." His relationship with Parritt, resulting in his direct responsibility for the suicide of the young man, makes Larry realize that he cannot
remain in the grandstand, that he will always look at the human scene "with
pity." And Hickey hacks away at Larry's pretense of wanting to die. At
play's end, Larry realizes that he is "the only real convert to death Hickey
made here." While the rest of the derelicts at Harry Hope's are pounding

their glasses and singing and laughing, Larry "stares in front of him, oblivious of their racket." Stripped of illusion, he is now dead, or ready to die. The others, returning to their illusions, can live. In between, we find Hickey, who leaves the stage to die, but remains with his illusion. All of which has important implications for a discussion of the play's genre.

At a rare press conference, prodded by his return to Broadway with the production of *The Iceman Cometh,* O'Neill said:

> There is a feeling around, or I'm mistaken, of fate. Kismet, the negative fate; not in the Greek sense. . . . It's struck me as time goes on, how something funny, even farcical, can suddenly without any apparent reason, break up into something gloomy and tragic. . . . A sort of unfair *non sequitur,* as though events, as though life, were being manipulated just to confuse us. I think I'm aware of comedy more than I ever was before; a big kind of comedy that doesn't stay funny very long. I've made some use of it in *The Iceman.* The first act is hilarious comedy, *I think,* but then some people may not even laugh. At any rate, the comedy breaks up and the tragedy comes on.

The quote offers a prophetic comment on the kind of "tragicomedy" written by Samuel Beckett and Friedrich Dürrenmatt, where the comedy veers toward tragedy. O'Neill's words accurately pinpoint the comedy of his play's first act, a comedy which persists in more sporadic fashion during the rest of the play. And his belief that comedy turns to tragedy is also accurate, but it needs some qualifying discussion.

The Iceman Cometh is a complex play, having received much critical attention precisely because it displays a rich ambiguity. That the title itself can be approached by way of the Bible and a crude joke, that the realistic atmosphere hearkens the symbolic, that the play, like Larry, looks at both sides of an issue, that the arrangement of characters seems schematic at the same time that the characters themselves display human anguish—all of these result in ambiguity of response. The derelicts have the *possibility* of tragedy because they are in a boundary situation, because they are victims of "negative fate," and because they endure, but at play's end they remain in a comic world because they continue their lives in illusion and alcohol, essentially asleep. Perhaps they realize, deep within, that their pipe dreams will never materialize, that tomorrow will never come, but their stance as chorus—functioning as a group through much of the play, ending as a group in song and laughter at play's end, and even uttering choric statements during Hickey's long confession—and their inability to confront the truth of their lives or ask the questions about life that tragedy demands make them more comic than tragic. Hickey's self-discovery during his confession, his momentary awareness of the horror of his deed, the deed itself, his mission of salvation which leads to the opposite—these help to make Hickey a tragic figure. But his pipe dream of insanity, his insistence that he loved Evelyn, diminishes his tragic stature; he will go to his death in illusion. Parritt goes to his death paying for his guilt, which is a tragic act, but his essential weakness as a character and the schematic nature of his parroting role preclude tragedy. Larry Slade, however, who thought he was without the illusions of the others, discovers that he too needed a pipe dream, and now, at play's end, hearing the "thud" of Parritt's body, he confronts the painful truth about himself, "the only real convert to death Hickey made here." He is above illusion; he faces life (which for him means death) unflinchingly; he ends the play staring at the skull of death. The shallow cynical Jaques of an *As You Like It* comic world has become Hamlet.

In a letter to Lawrence Langner, O'Neill states that *The Iceman Cometh* is "perhaps *the* best" play he has written because

> there are moments in it that suddenly strip the soul of a man stark naked, not in cruelty or moral superiority, but with an understanding compassion which sees him as a victim of the ironies of life and of himself. These moments are for me the depth of tragedy, with nothing more that can possibly be said.

For O'Neill, all the frequenters of Harry Hope's saloon are tragic because all are victims of life's manipulation. This is an arguable point, but no one will deny that O'Neill presents his characters with "understanding compassion." He is very close to these bums of his good old days at Jimmy the Priest's, and there is no doubt that he drew lovingly from his memory to portray them. Like Larry Slade, who seems to be O'Neill's view of himself, O'Neill has an instinctive sympathy for his fellow creatures. He also has an ear for their particular idioms, producing in *The Iceman Cometh* a "linguistic symphony" of dialects. The musical metaphor must be stressed because O'Neill took great pains with the arrangements of sound and the repetition of phrase in the play. (When an assistant director pointed out to O'Neill that he repeated the "pipe dream" idea eighteen separate times, O'Neill emphatically told him, "I *intended* it to be repeated eighteen times!") Much of Jose Quintero's success in directing the play in 1956 stemmed from his instinctive understanding of O'Neill's "musical" emphasis. Quintero explained that *The Iceman Cometh* "was not built as an orthodox play."

> It resembles a complex musical form, with themes repeating themselves with slight variation, as melodies do in a symphony. It is a valid device, though O'Neill has often been criticized for it by those who do not see the strength and depth of meaning the repetition achieves.
>
> My work was somewhat like that of an orchestra conductor, emphasizing rhythms, being constantly aware of changing tempos; every character advanced a different theme. The paradox was that for the first time as a director, I began to understand the meaning of precision in drama—and it took a play four and one-half hours long to teach me, a play often criticized as rambling and overwritten.

Quintero's statement is an effective answer to Eric Bentley's belief, shared by many critics, that the play "is far too long." (When Bentley directed a German-language version he cut about an hour from the play, mostly from Larry's speeches and Hugo Kalmar's.) The length is necessary not for development of character: the derelicts (except for Larry Slade) do not grow; that is the point, they remain frozen to their condition. The length helps to produce the atmosphere of stagnation and allows the repetitions to work on the audience's emotions. The play offers little physical movement, but it does "move" its themes from one character to the next, one group to another, and this requires time and orchestration. The musical metaphor tells us much about O'Neill's dramatic art, as it does when used to describe that other arranger of emotional effects, that other dramatist of stagnation, Chekhov.

Always the "literary" O'Neill as well as the nostalgic O'Neill, in *The Iceman Cometh* he draws not only from memory but also from Gorky's *The Lower Depths* and Ibsen's *The Wild Duck* and the Bible and Nietzsche and Strindberg. The last is especially felt in Hickey's confession, where the horror of marriage takes on a Strindbergian emphasis, but Strindberg also hovers over the marital agonies of Harry Hope and Jimmy Tomorrow. O'Neill's abiding interest in Greek drama surely inspired him to make the denizens of Hope's saloon a "chorus" (the word itself mentioned a number of times in the stage directions), serving similar functions to the Greek chorus, especially in their utterances during Hickey's confession. Perhaps Greek drama prodded O'Neill to observe the unities in *The Iceman Cometh* and in all his last plays. Certainly the device is perfect for a dramatist who wishes to lock his characters in the present while they talk of the past which produced that present, a dramatist who wishes to achieve an intensity of emotional effect. And perhaps a specific Greek tragedy, Sophocles' *Oedipus Rex,* gave O'Neill the idea of having a murder buried in the past revealed in stages, as is Hickey's murder of Evelyn, thereby building up suspense as the audience waits for the next revelation. (In this technique, Ibsen may have been as strong an influence.)

The Iceman Cometh, as a result of what was happening in the world and what was happening to O'Neill personally, contains a dark view of man's condition, and is a startling contrast to the play written just before the twelve-year silence, *Days without End.* No religious affirmations here, no faith in God, just the need of men to carry on as best they can with the help of illusion and alcohol *and* the willingness of men to uphold the dreams of others. The latter points to the play's positive qualities, the understanding compassion that the play evokes. Here again—as with the "Waiting for Hickey" and the repetition of phrases—a comparison with Beckett's *Waiting for Godot* seems apt, for the derelicts, like Didi and Gogo, frozen to their places and to the present time, looking forward to a tomorrow that never comes, do have each other and do endure. *The Iceman Cometh* seems to depart philosophically from the plays that O'Neill wrote previously, but this is not altogether true. Forces continue to work "behind life" to control men's lives, the past controls the present and future, frustration remains the condition of man, there is darkness behind the door, life seems a dirty trick, "hopeless hope" and alcohol remain important means for survival, the themes of love and death continue to dominate. But O'Neill's emphasis seems different, and his existential view of life seems more clear and more true, with O'Neill's method sharpening his meaning. The classical unities, the large cast of characters (offering a wide variety of dialects), the musical orchestration of words and effects, the graceful melding of the realistic and symbolic, the crude and the biblical, the four and one-half hours' playing time, the atmosphere of stagnation, the comedy-tragedy combination—all give *The Iceman Cometh* a density of texture and a truth to life that places it in a class by itself, different from O'Neill's preceding plays (although containing many similar themes and devices) and different from the plays that served as its models. In it O'Neill, like the Larry Slade of the play's last moments, seems to be staring directly at man's *existence;* perhaps only Shakespeare and Sophocles before him, and Beckett after him, have stared at it so unblinkingly. A stunning accomplishment.

A mixed critical reception, however, greeted its anticipated and widely publicized 1946 Theatre Guild production, which brought O'Neill back to Broadway after his long silence. The play had only a modest run of 136 performances, and was to be the last O'Neill play to be performed on

Broadway during his lifetime. Those who faulted the play mentioned its prosaic language, its schematic arrangements and, most often, its excessive length. Usually applauded were the direction of Eddie Dowling and the setting of Robert Edmond Jones. It took ten years for the play to be produced again, this time to almost unqualified approval. Jose Quintero's production in 1956, performed by a newly formed company, the Circle in the Square, in a former Greenwich Village nightclub before a small audience of two hundred, began the O'Neill revival, three years after O'Neill's death. It had the longest run of any O'Neill play ever, 565 performances. One can only speculate as to why the play was so successful this time. Perhaps it was the intimate setting, allowing the audience to feel it was part of Harry Hope's saloon; perhaps it was the sympathetic direction and acting; perhaps—and this may help to explain the great interest in O'Neill's other late plays since 1956—the times had changed and America was ready for an O'Neill who was ahead of his time. (1956 was the year that Beckett's *Waiting for Godot* came to Broadway.)

Jose Quintero was then an unknown director; this production would make him famous and would begin a long artistic relationship between Quintero and O'Neill. Quintero's understanding of the play's "musical" qualities has already been discussed, but perhaps one other quality should be stressed. Quintero, judging from the comments of actors who worked for him, directs O'Neill *emotionally;* although he is a highly articulate man, he does not allow the intellectual or cerebral to enter his discussion of the play with his actors. That is, the dramatist who appeals so powerfully to the emotions is being served by a director who also works from the emotions. For the part of Hickey, Quintero chose an actor who approaches his parts on the gut level and who seems, like Quintero, to have an instinctive affinity for O'Neill, Jason Robards, Jr. His Hickey made theatre history and will always be the model for comparison. Such a comparison was made in 1973, when the popular actor Lee Marvin played Hickey for the American Film Theatre production, directed by John Frankenheimer. The film offered a satisfying and competent rendition of the play. It could not give the play an immediacy that only the stage can offer, but it was admirably faithful to O'Neill's intention. Marvin's performance, however, was unrelievedly one-dimensional, giving Hickey none of the affability or irony or anguish the role demands. On the other hand, Robert Ryan, just before his death, in fact dying of cancer while playing the part, gave a memorable performance as Larry Slade, trying to remain aloof from the world around him but torturedly making contact with it, exposing his soul against his will. Fredric March played Harry Hope with great skill, Jeff Bridges perfectly captured Don Parritt's obnoxiousness and vulnerability, Bradford Dillman was a believably besotted and shaky Willie Oban, and the rest of the cast performed beautifully, successfully capturing this fine play on film for posterity. That *The Iceman Cometh* will continue to be produced in years to come, despite its length, there can be no doubt. It stands with *Long Day's Journey* as O'Neill's most substantial achievement, making most other plays by American playwrights seem "like so much damp tissue paper," to borrow George Jean Nathan's words in his review of the 1946 production.

Between his crowning achievements, *The Iceman Cometh* and *Long Day's Journey into Night,* the long plays set in 1912, O'Neill wrote *Hughie* (written 1940, performed 1958 in Sweden, 1964 in America), a one-act play set in the summer of 1928 between 3 and 4 A.M. in the dingy lobby of a third-rate hotel in midtown New York City. It was part of a projected cycle of six one-act plays to be collectively entitled *By Way of Obit*. O'Neill explained the plan of the cycle to George Jean Nathan: the main character would talk about a person who recently died to another person who would do little but listen.

> Via this monologue you get a complete picture of the person who has died—his or her whole life story—but just as complete a picture of the life and character of the narrator. And you also get by another means—a use of stage directions, mostly—an insight into the whole life of the person who does little but listen.

Of the cycle, only *Hughie* was fully completed and produced posthumously, first in Sweden, then in America under the direction of Jose Quintero, with Jason Robards, Jr. playing the lead role, Erie Smith. In his beginnings O'Neill wrote one-act plays, but decided to abandon the form because one act does not allow enough time to develop character. Here at the end of his career (and after writing some plays of marathon length), O'Neill returns to the one-act form, and manages to develop three characters—the two who appear on stage, Erie Smith and Charlie Hughes, and the one talked about, the dead night clerk, Hughie. Erie Smith, "a teller of tales," delivers what is essentially a monologue, interrupted only occasionally and briefly by Charlie Hughes. The monologue tells us much about the speaker Erie, and much about Hughie, who used to listen to Erie's tales. The stage directions tell us much about Charlie Hughes, whose similarity to Hughie—even the name is similar—gives us a deeper view of the dead Hughie. In a sense, we know more about the dead man "by way of obit" than about the two living men on stage, although all are rather full portraits.

Chronology

1888	October 16, in New York City, Eugene Gladstone O'Neill is born to James O'Neill, a well-known actor, and Ella Quinlan.
1902	O'Neill enters Betts Academy in Stamford, Connecticut.
1906–7	Attends Princeton.
1909	Marries Kathleen Jenkins; goes prospecting for gold in Honduras.
1910	Son Eugene Gladstone O'Neill, Jr., is born. O'Neill sails for Buenos Aires.
1912	Divorces Kathleen Jenkins. Begins work as a reporter for *New London Telegraph*. Publishes poetry. Enters Gaylord Farm, tuberculosis sanatorium, for a six-month stay.
1913	*A Wife for Life* and *The Web*, O'Neill's first plays, are copyrighted.
1914	O'Neill's father helps to pay for the publication of *Thirst*, a volume of five one-act plays.
1916	Provincetown Players produce *Bound East for Cardiff, Thirst,* and *Before Breakfast*.
1917	*Fog, The Sniper, In the Zone, The Long Voyage Home,* and *Ile* are produced.
1918	O'Neill marries Agnes Boulton and moves to Cape Cod. *The Rope, Where the Cross Is Made,* and *The Moon of the Carribbees* are produced.
1919	*The Dreamy Kid* is produced. Son Shane is born.
1920	*Beyond the Horizon* is produced, and wins the Pulitzer Prize. *Chris Christoferson* (first version of *Anna Christie*), *Exorcism, The Emperor Jones,* and *Diff'rent* produced.
1921	*Gold, The Straw,* and *Anna Christie* produced. *Anna Christie* wins Pulitzer Prize, O'Neill's second.
1922	*The First Man* and *The Hairy Ape* produced.

1924   *Welded, The Ancient Mariner, All God's Chillun Got Wings, S. S. Glencairn,* and *Desire under the Elms* are produced.

1925   *The Fountain* produced. Daughter Oona is born.

1926   *The Great God Brown* produced. O'Neill receives an honorary Litt.D. from Yale University.

1928   *Marco Millions, Strange Interlude,* and *Lazarus Laughed* are produced. Wins third Pulitzer for *Strange Interlude.* Divorces again.

1929   O'Neill marries Carlotta Monterey. *Dynamo* is produced. Moves to Le Plessis, France.

1931   *Mourning Becomes Electra* is produced.

1932   Returns to U.S. and builds Casa Genotta in Sea Island, Georgia.

1933   *Ah, Wilderness!* is produced.

1934   *Days without End* is produced.

1936   O'Neill wins the Nobel Prize for literature.

1937   Moves to California, where he builds Tao House.

1946   *The Iceman Cometh* is produced.

1947   O'Neill contracts Parkinson's Disease. *A Moon for the Misbegotten* is produced.

1950   Son Eugene dies.

1953   O'Neill develops pneumonia and dies on November 27 in Boston.

1956   *Long Day's Journey into Night* is produced. Jose Quintero revives *The Iceman Cometh.*

1957   *A Touch of the Poet* is produced.

1958   *Hughie* is produced.

1962   *More Stately Mansions* is produced.

Contributors

HAROLD BLOOM, Sterling Professor of the Humanities at Yale University, is the author of *The Anxiety of Influence, Poetry and Repression,* and many other volumes of literary criticism. His forthcoming study, *Freud: Transference and Authority,* attempts a full-scale reading of all of Freud's major writings. A MacArthur Prize Fellow, he is general editor of five series of literary criticism published by Chelsea House.

CYRUS DAY was Professor of English at the University of Delaware. He has edited *Songs of John Dryden* and *Songs of Thomas D'Urfey.*

ROBERT B. HEILMAN is the author of numerous distinguished works on the theater, including *The Great Stage, Tragedy and Melodrama,* and *Shakespeare; the Tragedies.*

TIMO TIUSANEN, Professor of Theatre Research at the University of Helsinki, is the author of *O'Neill's Scenic Images* and *Dürrenmatt, A Study in Plays, Prose, Theory.*

ROBERT C. LEE teaches at Northwestern University.

TRAVIS BOGARD is Professor of Dramatic Art at the University of California at Berkeley. His works include *Contour in Time: The Plays of Eugene O'Neill* and *Tragic Satire of John Webster.*

JEAN CHOTHIA is Fellow and Assistant Lecturer in English at Selwyn College, Cambridge. She is the author of *Forging a Language.*

JOHN ORR is the author of *Tragic Drama and Modern Society.*

NORMAND BERLIN is Professor of English at the University of Massachusetts. He is the author of *The Secret Cause: A Study of Tragedy.*

Bibliography

Alexander, Doris. *The Tempering of Eugene O'Neill*. New York: Harcourt, Brace & World, 1962.

Andreach, Robert J. "O'Neill's Women in *The Iceman Cometh*." *Renascence* 18 (1966): 89–98.

Arested, Sverre. "*The Wild Duck* and *The Iceman Cometh*." *Scandinavian Studies* 20 (1948): i–ii.

Blackburn, Clara. "Continental Influence on Eugene O'Neill's Expressionistic Dramas." *American Literature* 13 (1941): 109–33.

Brashear, William R. "The Wisdom of O'Neill's *Iceman*." *American Literature* 36 (1964): 180–88.

Brustein, Robert. *The Theatre of Revolt: An Approach to the Modern Drama*. Boston: Little, Brown, 1964.

Cargill, Oscar, N. Brylliom Fagin, and William J. Fisher, eds. *O'Neill and His Plays: Four Decades of Criticism*. New York: New York University Press, 1961.

Chabrowe, Leonard. *Ritual and Pathos*. Lewisburg, Pa.: Bucknell University Press, 1976.

Driver, Tom F. "On the Late Plays of Eugene O'Neill." *Tulane Drama Review* 3, no. 2 (1958): 8–20.

Engel, Edwin. *Haunted Heroes of O'Neill*. Cambridge: Harvard University Press, 1953.

Falk, Doris V. *Eugene O'Neill and the Tragic Tension*. New Brunswick, N.J.: Rutgers University Press, 1958.

Floyd, Virginia, ed. *Eugene O'Neill at Work: Newly Released Ideas for Plays*. New York: Frederick Ungar, 1981.

Frazer, Winifred D. *Love as Death in* The Iceman Cometh. Gainesville: University of Florida Press, 1967.

Frenz, Horst, and Susan Tuck. *Eugene O'Neill's Critics: Voices from Abroad*. Carbondale: Southern Illinois University Press, 1984.

Gassner, John, ed. *O'Neill: A Collection of Critical Essays*. Englewood Cliffs, N.J.: Prentice-Hall, 1964.

Gelb, Arthur, and Barbara Gelb. *O'Neill*. New York: Harper & Row, 1962.

Long, Chester Clayton. *The Role of Nemesis in the Structure of Selected Plays by Eugene O'Neill*. The Hague: Mouton, 1968.

Quintero, Jose. "Postscript to a Journey." *Theatre Arts* 41 (1957): 27–29.

Raleigh, John Henry. *The Plays of Eugene O'Neill.* Carbondale: Southern Illinois University Press, 1965.

Robinson, James A. *Eugene O'Neill and Oriental Thought: A Divided Vision.* Carbondale: Southern Illinois University Press, 1983.

Sievers, W. David. *Freud on Broadway; A History of Psychoanalysis and the American Drama.* New York: Hermitage House, 1955.

Silverberg, William V. "Notes on *The Iceman Cometh.*" *Psychiatry* 10, no. 1 (February 1947): 27–29.

Sproxton, Birk. "Eugene O'Neill: Masks and Demons." *Sphinx* 3 (1975): 57–62.

Strickland, Edward. "Baudelaire's 'Portrait de Maitresses' and O'Neill's *The Iceman Cometh.*" *Romance Notes* 22 (1982): 291–94.

Törnquist, Egil. *A Drama of Souls: Studies in O'Neill's Super-Naturalistic Technique.* New Haven: Yale University Press, 1969.

Trilling, Lionel. "Eugene O'Neill." *The New Republic* 86, no. 1138 (September 1936): 176–79.

Valgamae, Mardi. "O'Neill and German Expressionism." *Modern Drama* 10 (1967): 111–23.

Watson, James. "The Theater in *The Iceman Cometh:* Some Modernist Implications." *Arizona Quarterly* 34 (1978): 230–38.

Weissman, Philip, M.D. "Conscious and Unconscious Autobiographical Dramas of Eugene O'Neill." *Journal of the American Psychoanalytic Association* 5 (1957): 432–60.

Acknowledgments

"The Iceman and the Bridegroom" by Cyrus Day from *Modern Drama* 1, no. 1 (May 1958), © 1958 by A. C. Edwards. Reprinted by permission of *Modern Drama*.

"The Drama of Disaster" by Robert B. Heilman from *Tragedy and Melodrama: Versions of Experience* by Robert B. Heilman, © 1968 by the University of Washington Press. Reprinted by permission.

"Composition for Solos and a Chorus: *The Iceman Cometh*" by Timo Tiusanen from *O'Neill's Scenic Images* by Timo Tiusanen, © 1968 by Princeton University Press. Reprinted by permission.

"Evangelism and Anarchy in *The Iceman Cometh*" by Robert C. Lee from *Modern Drama* 12, no. 2 (September 1969), © 1969 by A. C. Edwards. Reprinted by permission of *Modern Drama*.

"The Door and the Mirror: *The Iceman Cometh*" by Travis Bogard from *Contour in Time: The Plays of Eugene O'Neill* by Travis Bogard, © 1972 by Oxford University Press. Reprinted by permission.

"The Late Plays and the Development of 'Significant Form': *The Iceman Cometh*" by Jean Chothia from *Forging a Language: A Study of the Plays of Eugene O'Neill* by Jean Chothia, © 1979 by Cambridge University Press. Reprinted by permission.

"*The Iceman Cometh* and Modern Society" (originally entitled "Eugene O'Neill II: The Life Remembered") by John Orr from *Tragic Drama and Modern Society* by John Orr, © 1981 by John Orr. Reprinted by permission of Macmillan Press Ltd. and Barnes & Noble Books.

"Endings" by Normand Berlin from *Eugene O'Neill* by Normand Berlin, © 1982 by Normand Berlin. Reprinted by permission of Macmillan Press Ltd. and Grove Press.

Index